Living the Abundant Life

Michele Michaels

Foreword by
Erin Thiele

RestoreMinistries.net

NarrowRoad Publishing House

Living the Abundant Life
Michele Michaels

Published by:
Editorial NarrowRoad
POB 830
Ozark, MO 65721 U.S.A.

The materials from Restore Ministries were written for the sole purpose of encouraging women. For more information, visit us at:

RMIEW.com
EncouragingWomen.org
RestsoreMinistries.net

Unless otherwise indicated, most Scripture verses are taken from the *New American Standard Bible* (NASB). Scripture quotations marked KJV are taken from the *King James Version* of the Bible, and Scripture quotations marked NIV are taken from the *New International Version*. Our ministry is not partial to any particular version of the Bible but **love** them all so that we are able to help every woman in any denomination who needs encouragement.

Tenth Revised Edition

Copyright © 2019 by Michele Michaels and Erin Thiele

Cover Design by Dallas and Tara Thiele
First Printing: 2016
Second Printing: 2019
ISBN: 1-931800-53-7
ISBN 13: 978-1-931800-53-2
Library of Congress Control Number: 2019908986

Table of Contents

1. Could *this* be His Plan?....................................5

2. Giving is the Secret...14

3. The Wave of Adversity.....................................24

4. When Do I Give Up?..35

5. Small as a Man's Fist.......................................41

6. That Amazing Grace..47

7. Believing God for Great Things.........................53

8. You're Being Set-Up..57

9. What's the Point?..63

10. From the Inside Out...69

11. Guilty of All...78

12. Every Encumbrance...83

13. Those Voices..89

14. You're Beautiful!!..93

15. Utterly Lovesick...98

16. No Longer an Adulteress................................105

About the Author..116

Foreword

It's been years since the Feminist Movement robbed women out of their rightful roles and blessings of how God designed women to be. Though it's goal was to give women the same rights as men, it has served to cause women to have no choice but to become single mothers, provide not only for themselves but often their male cohabitant. Women have not freed themselves from men, as it said it was set out to accomplish, but instead, women have become obsessed with having a man, any man at any cost. Not surprisingly the Bible's prophet said times like this would come. Isaiah 4:1 The Message (MSG) says, "That will be the day when seven women will gang up on one man, saying, 'We'll take care of ourselves, get our own food and clothes. Just give us a child. Make us pregnant so we'll have something to live for!"

It's women like *Michele who have been called to blaze the trails for women who will soon find themselves, alone, without a husband or children or family. In this five book series, Michele takes us along on her journey that didn't lead to her regaining what she lost, but finding a relationship so strong, so fulfilling and so peaceful that she is an inspiration to all of us.

Much of what I read in this book, when it was first only available to women in her church, I've used to help the women in my own ministry. Each of us needs to glean the unspoken truths, wisdom and freedom that Michele has experienced and has shared with us in this dynamic book for women.

I'm honored to call Michele my friend, and it's through what she has transparently shared with us in this book that will help us each discover how we can rise above every situation He calls us to go through.

Erin Thiele
Restore Ministries International

Chapter 1

Could *this* be His Plan?

The Rock! His work is perfect,
For all His ways are just;
A God of faithfulness and without injustice,
Righteous and upright is He.
—Deuteronomy 32:4

There was no question that God was going to have me write about the last few weeks of my life. Though difficult beyond measure, and while I am deep in the midst of it, I have to say that it has been exciting. Just a week ago, I would not have described my trials as "exciting," but once again, God has gotten a hold of me (at my request), and once again, I am changed (by my Heavenly Husband and His perfect love towards me).

Right now, I am on a tiny propeller plane headed for Miami; it's my second flight with thirteen more to go before I arrive back home more than a month from now. I am looking forward to meeting RMI members once I arrive in Miami, and to see what He has planned. It is going to be exciting. The excitement has escalated due to the fact that another airline that was supposed to bring me to Brazil tomorrow has just declared bankruptcy, so my flight was cancelled.

Not too much trouble for God, but it does take tapping into Him in order to secure the faith that I'll need so that I don't, instead, turn to a state of panic rather than remain excited about what's up ahead.

This is all due to God who has changed me. God changed me through stretching me to the point that I told Him that I was about to snap. He told me that I wouldn't, so I stopped being concerned. Instead of delivering me, He simply reminded me that this was all necessary in order for me to be ready for what He has planned for me up ahead. I know it is big, He told me, but the details are still more like a dream, a silly dream, that no one would believe—not even me—and I believe there will be some really crazy, yet amazing things before whatever He has planned for me happens.

"Look among the nations! Observe! Be astonished! Wonder! Because I am doing something in your days—You would not believe if you were told" (Habakkuk 1:5).

God versus Jesus

May I interject something here? Most Christians believe that you can interchange God and Jesus, Father and Husband due to these simply being "names" of the same Person. I hope you know that I'm not concerned with trying to debate religious beliefs or doctrine, my aim is to simply help each woman receive everything that's been denied her. So the truth is this, if you need a husband, Jesus wants more than anything to be your Husband. Simply speak to Him as you would the most amazingly-in-love-with-you Man of your dreams. If you also need a Father, maybe because you never had a father or a good father or your father left you (he deserted, neglected or even passed away), 6then speak to God, the Father that way. With this understanding, when I felt myself being stretched, I knew it was my Father, God, who was doing the stretching. My Husband isn't like that, especially since we're on an eternal honeymoon.

If you doubt this is true, just try it out. Begin to realize there's a lot more to Who cares for you than you've been told. It's not just One Person, and there's proof throughout the Bible. Here's one, in this verse God spoke: "Let us make human beings in our image, make them reflecting our nature..." Genesis 1:26. The Lord also said something in Isaiah 6:8, "Then I heard the voice of the Lord, saying, 'Whom shall I send, and who will go for **Us**?" References to Us and We are all throughout the Bible, and due to not understanding, the church has felt obligated to interpret what they've named the Trinity, and the different denominations have all voiced strong opinions on the subject over centuries.

Unfortunately, most were inaccurate, due to the fact that you simply can't explain something as powerful, and especially because it's impossible to do if you haven't first experienced it, because it's a relationship they're trying to explain. It's like a woman trying to explain what it feels like to be a mother who hasn't been a mother. You can't explain how you'll change, not until you've also experienced being a mother. How can you explain? And when you try to explain, it's impossible, because it's not able to be understood or comprehended by the mind. It can only be experienced through the heart. So too, experiencing God's Son as your Husband, and also God as a Father who loved you enough to give you His Son, and therefore also loves you enough to help change you and to help you continue to grow by stretching you. So now I've had my say, let's return to what I was sharing with you...

There is no doubt that what is ahead for me will change my life and all those around me, but this chapter, dear bride, is not about me, it is about you. God wants to change *your* life as well, but to do that He has to stretch you, and the only way to do that is to bring really incredible trials into your life in order to stretch your faith and trust in Him. This is just God's way. It is not until this principle is understood, which means you've embraced it, that you'll actually come to the point that you're excited by what's thrown at you because you will then be able to receive what He wants to give you, the way He gives. But we can't understand it, until we're willing to work *with* and work *through* this principle, rather than fight against it.

Without realizing it, the church has been made to believe (myself included) that anything that has happened to us, or happens to us, which wasn't or isn't an *obvious* blessing, was/is an attack **by the enemy** that we are required to fight against. Yet, what I found out through many, many trials, tribulations and crises was that most of these "attacks" were simply God's way of directing my path, helping to stretch me in order to bless me, and that I had been fighting against God and it was not the enemy at all. Yes, I know and believe that there *is* an adversary, the Bible tells us that, but I think that this little guy gets way too much attention when he is really powerless in the life of the believer who is sold out for Jesus.

Let me give you an example of this. Earlier this year, while on my way to Europe, I missed my connecting flight (because my plane landed too late), and I found myself on a very small propeller plane (God has such a sense of humor and is determined to break the yoke of my dislike of flying no matter what it takes). This was not, as it turned out, the enemy blocking me from my speaking engagement in Geneva, Switzerland. As it turned out, it was actually God directing me so that I would not merely speak to a small group of women (my choice), but by missing my connecting flight, forcing me to take a prop plan *through* the Alps rather than simply fly *over* these magnificent mountains— I would know that it was He who wanted me to speak to the entire church (His plan), which included men (whom I did **not** want to speak to).

"As the heavens are **higher** than the earth, so are my **ways higher** than your **ways** and my thoughts than your thoughts" (Isaiah 55:9).

Though I know this verse above backwards and forwards, I am still amazed how each time I read it and meditate on it, the power of its message becomes more real as I live each day by faith. Our thoughts and our plans are so inferior and so beneath the plans that God has for us. That is why my prayer life has completely changed, because I finally know that for me to stipulate what I want (making a detailed list) only complicates my life. Instead, my desire is to simply walk out His plan for my life. No longer do I have the need to be a part of His planning meeting. So instead of prayer, I simply enjoy talking to my Husband: I tell Him how I'm feeling and try to remember to sit quietly because very often He has something He wants to tell me too. But no longer am I eager to tell Him (or worse, beg Him) for what I want or need because I have all I want and all I need in Him.

At the same time, I must also explain that what happens when you choose to trust Him at this level is that nothing at all appears to work out *simply* and/or *perfectly* any more. Once you just let God be God and allow His will to be done, it inevitably appears that you have missed Him completely. It is impossible for me to count the number of times that I asked myself over the course of these past few weeks, "Could *this* be His plan?"

For instance, on the morning that I left for my around-the-world tour, I stopped at the bank to draw out some cash as I would normally do. Most people will tell you that it is dangerous to carry cash (and especially when you're traveling where I am headed), but that makes no difference to me. I would rather live dangerously in the physical world than to live dangerously in the spiritual realm, which is when we choose safety, convenience or what we would rather do than to do what God tells us to do. The interesting thing is that by drawing out this simple sum of money, it just about cleaned out all my bank accounts. Interesting. Wouldn't this mean that it wasn't His plan? Would His plan put me and my family in a precarious position?

Another example was just five days before I left, I not only noticed that I would soon be totally out of money in all my accounts, but I did not have my around-the-world tickets, nor did I have my passport nor my visa for Africa—the list was endless. That Monday morning, when I made this ominous list in my head, I could feel my negative emotions trying to take over. So I told the Lord, "Honey, I really need more of You right now." Remember, we don't need to plead or beg or ask for any "thing" specific, instead, I knew that what I needed (and what you always need) is more of Him. Nevertheless, no matter how many times I said that, the emotions continued to overwhelm me. That's when I realized that there is no perfect "formula" and what He was leading me to do is to simply ask Him what I should do next in order to feel more at peace. This was when He led me out to my deck, coffee in hand, and no Bible—so that He could just talk to me.

Once seated, He told me to think of the "worst case scenario," which was that without travel documents and money, I just couldn't go; instantly, my "worst case scenario" became my *best case* scenario! I would gladly forfeit all the time and money invested in this trip just to stay home with my children. Yet, this possibility lasted just 24 hours. Later that day while driving that still small voice of the Lord (that I have come to know and love) told me, "You know, you *are* going." Though I hate to admit it, tears welled up in my eyes because I didn't want to go. Even though I didn't respond the way I may have wanted, even then, He loved me just as much. Do you know that? The Lord is not disappointed in you, He is not mad at you, He is not going to punish you—He loves you more than you could ever know.

Within a matter of just 72 hours, all impossibilities became possible because it was His will and His plan for me to go, and it was by stretching me that He was able to teach me just a little more about trusting Him. My tickets arrived, my visa came in the mail for Kenya and my passport arrived just in time. Each impossibility on my list was accomplished because He is God.

"Behold, I am the LORD, the God of all flesh; is anything too difficult for Me?" (Jeremiah 32:27).

The Plot Thickens and I am Still Smiling

Today is Monday, three days into my tour, and I am walking the streets of Miami dragging 100 pounds (46 kilograms) of luggage (due to carrying RMI books) while the plane that I was booked on is (at this very moment) flying over Venezuela. The airline I mentioned earlier that was to take me to Brazil left without me, because while trying to book me on another airline (remember, the one I was on declared bankruptcy), that's when the ticket agent asked me for my Brazilian visa. Interestingly, I did not possess one; I didn't even know I needed one. So I spoke to the Lord about what to do next and He pointed me to go over to get a coffee and a couple of donuts. Don't you love this Man of ours?!?! At the café, I shared a table with a traveling emergency room nurse who was eager to hear about Jesus, my new Husband.

We spoke for a full two hours, which I was concerned to be doing, but remember, I'd made my list of "worst case scenarios" that could mean I only made a short trip to Miami and I could forget South America, Africa and Europe. Oh heavens, how wonderful that would be!

What I didn't know is that He led me to wait because the Brazilian consulate's office wasn't yet opened. Once I left the airport the situation turned a bit crazy because it meant that I had just forty minutes to get to the office, fill out the paperwork, and submit my application. At the time I didn't know that it takes at least a week for it to be approved, but thankfully He kept me in the dark about this fact. So, after hailing a cab, I headed downtown (a thirty-minute drive) while my RMI hostess headed to the post-office to get a money order for a hundred dollars since they said they would not accept cash.

Though I got there within five minutes of the office closing, my hostess (while en route) was called away on, would you believe, another emergency? And with no money order, it meant no visa. Could this be God's plan? I had just one day to leave the U.S. and get to Brazil, or I would miss my flight to Johannesburg, South Africa. With every opposition coming against me, God made a way where there was no way—my visa, I was told, would be ready between noon and one p.m. the very next day. However, the airline, as I said, was bankrupt, and its reservation line had been disconnected. Still, I knew that if God wanted me to get to Brazil and to keep traveling, He would make a way—but, again, who wouldn't ask, could this be God's plan? And I had to ask myself, "Isn't it just possible that I missed God?"

So this means it's time for a Word booster:

"I, the LORD, **search** the **heart,** I test the mind, even to give to each man according to his ways, according to the results of his deeds" (Jeremiah 17:10).

"For the eyes of the LORD move to and fro throughout the earth that He may strongly support those whose **heart** is **completely** His" (2 Chronicles 19:9).

So, no, this means, no, you didn't miss God, and neither did I! When things don't fall into place perfectly, it does not mean that we've missed God, or that He has abandoned us. It simply means that He is bringing us up to a higher level of faith and trust in Him. Remember . . .

"Now **faith** is the assurance of things **hoped for,** the conviction of *things not seen"* (Heb. 11:1). "For we walk by faith, not by sight . . ." (2 Corinthians 5:7).

"I have told you these things, so that in me you may have peace. In this world **you *will* have trouble.** But take heart! I have *overcome* the world" (John 16:33 NIV).

The point is this, whether I got to South America, South Africa, Kenya or the Netherlands on this tour was not the point. The point is that I loved Him enough to pack my bags, leave my children for five weeks, and go. This is all He asks of you and me.

• Will you go when He leads?

• Will you trust Him enough to get out of your comfort zone and be willing to hear that still small voice even when it looks as if you are headed the wrong way down a one-way street?

I am—how about you?

So, what about all those people whom you know that will mock and ridicule you for living like this? Well, that happens when you're trusting God, right? Just look at Nehemiah trying to rebuild the temple in Nehemiah 4.

We only need to look at Who always writes the last chapter to know that He promises that we will not be ashamed. In the end, the humble (those who trust Him and are willing to look foolish for Him) will be exalted. Though, in the midst, *others* will jeer and mock and scream at you, "Where is your God now?" Yet, we know that He will eventually show up; yet, sometimes He *is* late. Oh, sorry, does that rock your boat?

I know that you and I have all heard that God is *never* late, but that is just not true. Remember, Jesus was late on purpose when his good friend Lazarus was sick. He actually let His good friend die on purpose. That's because God loves to write the last chapter—the sort of chapter that makes us want to jump up and down and let out a shout of praise! Instead of just healing a sick person, Jesus takes this miracle over the top and raises His friend, the one wrapped in grave clothes—He raised Lazarus from the dead!

Is that how you are feeling now, dead? Is your miracle, your promise, your vision, your around-the-world tour dead... is it dead in the grave? Yes, it may certainly look dead, maybe you're sure it IS dead, but— the same raising-from-the-dead power that raised Lazarus, that raised Jesus, still works today. God loves to stack the odds, back us into the Red Sea with our enemies in hot pursuit, and also to be sure to gather all the mockers around so that everyone, everyone, will know that He is God—the Creator of the earth. Time and circumstance are in His hand. So when it doesn't make sense to us, we only need to remember that His ways are so much above our ways, and just when you think you have figured God out, He'll show you that there is much more to Him than you knew.

There is more love, more compassion, more forgiveness, and much more that He has in store for you as you enjoy your journey on this abundant life that begins once you surrender your life to Him and agree to go along with Him in faith.

Yes, I guess, this IS His plan.

Chapter 2

Giving is the Secret

Give, and it will be given to you.
They will pour into your lap a good measure—
pressed down, shaken together, and running over.
For by your standard of measure
it will be measured to you in return.
—Luke 6:38

This morning, as I do every morning since I've been living my abundant life, I was excited to discover the new revelation that the Lord was going to show me. So with my Bible and coffee in hand, anticipation was flowing through me to the point where I couldn't wait for Him to share a new, hidden secret to me just as it says in Isaiah 48:6 that He would do, "I proclaim to you new things from this time, even hidden things which you have not known."

Heart beating wildly, opening my Bible, I asked the Lord where, what verse, He wanted me to open to. He began leading me through a series of verses that are not just for me, but for each and every one of you who have yearned and wanted to know the secret to abundance. Not surprisingly the secret is—**giving.**

"'Behold, days are coming,' declares the LORD, 'When the plowman will overtake the reaper and the treader of grapes him who sows seed; when the mountains will drip sweet wine and all the hills will be dissolved. Also I will restore the captivity of My people Israel, And they will rebuild the ruined cities and live in them; They will also plant vineyards and drink their wine, And make gardens and eat their fruit. I will also plant them on their land, and they will not again be rooted out from their land which I have given them,' Says the LORD your God" (Amos 9:13–15).

Next He led me to, "Then the LORD answered me and said, 'Record the vision and inscribe it on tablets, that the one who reads it may run. For the vision is yet for the appointed time; it hastens toward the goal and it will not fail, though it tarries, wait for it; for it will certainly come, it will not delay'" (Habakkuk 2:2–3). So with my computer open, I began to document, to record and inscribe these truths, knowing too, that what He's told me and envisioned will certainly come just as it said. Then I continued reading...

"Look among the nations! Observe! Be astonished! Wonder! Because I am doing something in your days—**You would not believe if you were told**" (Habakkuk 1:5).

Skipping a few verses, He next had me read: "Though the fig tree should not blossom and there be no fruit on the vines, though the yield of the olive should fail and the fields produce no food, Though the flock should be cut off from the fold and there be no cattle in the stalls, yet I will exult in the LORD, I will rejoice in the God of my salvation. The Lord GOD is my strength, and He has made my feet like hinds' feet, and makes me walk on my high places" (Habakkuk 3:17–19).

What the Lord is telling you in this verse, those of you who have had a heart for giving, and also what He has been speaking to me, is that we are on the threshold of some amazing things that are going to happen in our lives! As He put it that morning, He said, "You would not believe if you were told"! And He ends by saying that even though right now we see nothing, by faith, we must continue to praise Him.

So, now that I've recorded the vision, it's time for us to explore this wonderful revelation even more, so we can fully grasp this truth in order to remain in a constant state of praise!

It is so easy for me to believe these promises the Lord unveiled to me this morning, because, as I look back at my life *now* in comparison to where I was just one year ago, it's not as difficult to see the impossibility of it really happening. For instance, prior to me finding the abundant life, I never ventured much out of my house, but instead, stayed mostly in my own room where I worked, and never even ventured downstairs. Downstairs to our family room, or the boys' bedrooms, and also where my husband's office was once located. That was a just year ago.

This morning I will head downstairs to *my* new office, while I begin completing plans to take my second trip around the world—visiting places that I had read about but didn't even know where they were on the map—and even visiting countries that I didn't know existed. Last year, if the Lord told me that all of this would happen over the course of just one year, I "would not believe if I were told"!

Whatever is about to happen this year is also going to be life-changing; not just in my life, but also my children's lives, my ministry's future, each of the lives of women whom my life touches, and your life too (which is why He's led you to read this book). As a result, what is about to happen in your life will also touch every life that your life touches. You see, that's the point: God touches our lives in order for us to touch other lives and to cause that ripple to spread His love, His truths to countless hurting souls who are desperately in need of Him. This, dear friend, is a revelation that you need to grab hold of and hide deep in your heart: **God *gives* to us in order for us to *give* to others—that's the secret to living abundantly.**

In the same way and to the same measure as He *gave* us His Son, who now is our beloved Husband, who has loved us in such a way as to heal our hearts and make us feel cleaned, cherished and in need of no one and nothing else but Him, others desperately need Him as well. So this means we cannot keep Him or His love to ourselves, but we must *give* this gift of His Son, sharing Him with others. He wants to be to each woman we meet, the same Lover, Healer, Provider and Protector, which will happen—once our lives shine so brightly that everyone we meet *asks* us about our shining hope within us!

That's why it's important to be prepared for how you'll answer *when* others **ask**, as it says we are to do in First Peter 3:15 NIV, "Always be prepared to give an answer to everyone who asks you to give the reason for the hope that you have. But do this with gentleness and respect." Reading it in the Message Bible it says it this way, "Be ready to speak up and tell anyone who asks why you're living the way you are, and always with the utmost courtesy." You need to respect that not everyone is ready to know Him, so your goal is to simply share *your* hope, and what has changed *you,* making sure you wait until you're asked. Also, having a heart that is not trying to push anything on anyone, women especially will witness your shining love to them and others to the point that each will naturally be drawn to wanting to experience what you have, and what you possess is Him.

Dear friend, each time God reveals mysteries to us, like revealing to us that we have a Husband who loves us as much as He does, it's in order that we reveal these mysteries and truth to others, by living in such a way that our lives speak volumes and then giving them the truth when they ask. "You are our letter, written in our hearts, known and read by all men" (2 Corinthians 3:2). This is the correct and true form of "witnessing"—it's others *witnessing* our lives, not by confronting others. Our Husband showers us with blessings and love so we can in turn radiate His love and shower others with His blessings and His love. This is the secret—giving what He's given to us.

Blessings will Overtake You

Going back to the first verse where the Lord told me, "'Behold, days are coming,' declares the LORD, 'When the plowman will **overtake** the reaper and the treader of grapes him who sows seed . . ." this, too, is something that happens almost every day of my life, and will in yours—if you have learned the secret, which is giving what He's given to you.

What I understood this verse to mean is totally different from what I have now come to understand it to mean. The word "overtake" when running the race of life means that the blessing gets to the finish line **before** we do. "Therefore, since we have so great a cloud of witnesses surrounding us, let us also lay aside every encumbrance and the sin which so easily entangles us, and let us *run with endurance the race that is set before us*, **fixing our eyes on Jesus,** the author and perfecter of faith, who for the joy set before Him endured the cross, despising the shame, and has sat down at the right hand of the throne of God. For consider Him who has endured such hostility by sinners against Himself, so that you will not grow weary and lose heart" (Hebrews 12:1–3).

Some years ago, whenever trials hit me and my life, I began to believe that something good was going to come out of it—but some day— some year or some decade later. Yet, over the course of this past year I began to look for that blessing not a year or a decade later, but to look for the blessing immediately; immediately *after* the trial was *over*. Then, that's exactly what began to happen. The day arrived when all that I had sown began to *overtake* me and would often show up even before the trial even hit my life. Money showed up in my hand or wallet or bank account *before* I needed it. Plans for what I needed to do showed up *before* anyone had even asked me the question.

Then, as I said, whenever God revealed a new truth to me, *giving* me something wonderful to walk towards, I then began to live that truth and would *give* the same truth to others. And since my children are those who are closest to me, and they too are my inheritance that will continue to give to others when I'm gone, I often am led to *give* truths to my children first. The principle of our blessings overtaking us was one such principle.

It happened the day my niece was flying back home, we needed to drive to an airport more than three hours away, so my brother offered to pay for us to spend the night in a hotel near the airport. Oh the favor of God. On our way there, we were driving through a small city in the middle of nowhere when my daughter leans up and whispers, "Mama, I'm so sorry but I just remembered I forgot to pack my swimsuit. I'm so sorry!!" and I could tell she was nearly in tears since we'd selected our hotel based on their amazing pool and hot tub. Immediately I assured her that there was no reason to worry, fear or feel badly, but to instead get excited because His blessings would overtake us! Without exaggerating, I turned my head and looked to my right to see a small Walmart; immediately I took a quick right turn explaining that He obviously wanted to bless her with a new swimsuit! Then paraphrasing Isaiah 40:2, "Speak kindly . . . And call out to her, that her warfare has ended, that her iniquity has been removed, that she has received of the LORD'S hand DOUBLE for all her sins [or mistakes]." Even though swimsuit season had passed, sure enough, as we walked in, right near the front of the store my daughter found one of the cutest swimsuits I'd ever seen AND it was beyond anointed. This swimsuit lasted for several summers and was even in good enough shape to pass down to her sister, which fit her just as perfectly. Only God could do this!

Not only did my daughters walk away from this experience with an understanding of how blessings overtake us, but to be sure to look for the blessings immediately, something He first *gave* to me. But remember, my niece was also with us, so she took this back and shared it, by her living it with her sister and her parents!! This ripple of His love for us spread half way around the world!!

To Embrace Waiting

Now to move on and discuss that infamous and also loathed principle of waiting. Wow, has the Lord given me knew insight into this principle too!

If you are anything like how I used to be, I simply **hated,** loathed, and squirmed when I was *forced* to wait. Now, I am thrilled when I'm asked to wait, since I know now that waiting is an exciting part of His plan. Why? What has changed? The revelation that was always there in Scripture but I never really wanted to embrace it: "Yet those who **wait** for the LORD will gain *new* **strength**; they will mount up with wings like eagles, they will run and not get tired, they will walk and not become weary" (Isaiah 40:31).

Now I have gained enough experience to know that when I'm required to wait for something, anything, it's because God has orchestrated that period of waiting so that it will give me the time I need to "gain new strength" so I will "not get tired or grow weary" when the new blessing shows up in my life. Waiting also signals to me, telling me that what is up ahead is going to need more strength (physically, mentally, emotionally, and/or spiritually) than what I have at the present time. Therefore, I am more than happy to wait and use that time to build my strength with pure excitement—the strength that will carry me through whatever wave I am about to ride. This is a good metaphor or picture of how to benefit from adversity, as this is how God created our world and how we, as His bride, are able to live abundantly.

Waves of Adversity

Another revelation was that for years I swam *into* the waves of my life only to eventually become weary and defeated. Yet, over the course of just one year, I learned the secret to overcome these waves of adversity differently, by no longer resisting evil and each time something or someone comes against me, I need to instead turn around and ride along with the adversity because God wants to bring me up higher, living even more abundantly. Remember, "He has made my feet like hinds' feet, and makes me walk on my high places" (Habakkuk 3:19). It actually happened by me living out the often neglected Beatitudes found in the book of Matthew. Most stop reading after He lists all the "blessed are you" but instead, just keep reading and grasp an even greater truth, when Jesus later on says...

"But I say to you, do *not* resist an evil person; but whoever slaps you on your right cheek, turn the other to him also. If anyone wants to sue you and take your shirt, let him have your coat also. Whoever forces you to go one mile, go with him two. Give to him who asks of you, and do not turn away from him who wants to borrow from you. You have heard that it was said, 'YOU SHALL LOVE YOUR NEIGHBOR and hate your enemy.' **But I say to you,** love your enemies and pray for those who persecute you, so that you may be sons of your Father who is in heaven; for He causes His sun to rise on the evil and the good, and sends rain on the righteous and the unrighteous" (Matthew 5: 39–45).

Riding the wave of adversity means that you go **with** the flow, never opposing it. Jesus explained how we are to react when people tell you to do something, but this is far from what the church tells us. Yet Jesus made it a point to document what He said, *"But I say to you . . . "* So like everyone ignorant of the truth, I resisted evil, and made sure I never stood close enough to anyone who'd once slapped me. I would avoid seeing them and if I was forced to see them, I'd stand back emotionally. And I certainly didn't **do** *more* or **give** *more* than what someone asked me to give them; therefore, I continued to miss the blessings of His message and the secret to living abundantly and powerfully—by giving—especially to those who hurt or use us.

What changed was that after finding my abundant life, I began getting what I needed directly from God like wisdom, and directly from the Lord, like the love that I desperately needed. So once I got what they each gave me, I was finally able to give what was lavished upon me to others. Once I received so much love and acceptance from the Lord (when I fully became His bride), then any evil person who wanted to slap me (emotionally by their words or by actions) no longer hurt me at all. After a while, each slap was just a wake-up call alerting me that I was about to go up higher again, and that meant that the Lord was going to ask me to *give* more than what was asked—giving to those who hurt and wanted to use me, which is when the huge blessings come—when the person you're giving to doesn't deserve it!

Giving is incredibly powerful when it is demanded, stolen, or asked for unkindly. Adversity, I now understand, is actually the fuel we need, or like watering the seed that will bring about a bountiful harvest that He has promised us. So, with this truth understood, it's now very easy to embrace adversity rather than running from it or pushing my way through it. And keep this in mind when your crops, your fields are not producing fruits. If you don't water them, or if you don't put fuel in your spiritual engine, is it any wonder why you are not moving forward? Read this verse:

"Therefore I am **well content** with weaknesses, with insults, with distresses, with persecutions, with difficulties, for Christ's sake; for when I am weak, then I am strong" (2 Corinthians 12:10). "Not that I speak from want, for I have *learned* to be **content** in *whatever* circumstances I am" (Philippians 4:11). To be honest, I was never content with anything close to difficulties or persecutions, only because I hadn't been open to or knew that I needed to openly receive what God and my Husband wanted to give me. Then, once I took it, absorbed it, lived it, and then **gave** it, only then was I able to be "**content** in *whatever* circumstances" I was in.

Root of Evil: Love of Money

One area that I have learned to embrace this principle of *giving* is in the area of *giving* money. We are all so fearful of not having enough that we foolishly withhold what we have, due to the love of money, only to find that our fears are realized and will then happen. What we fear actually happens because it's manifested or created because of and due to our fears. How true this verse is to me now that I have learned the secret of giving, especially in giving to and blessing my enemies: "There is one who scatters, and yet increases all the more, and there is one who withholds what is justly due, and yet it results only in want" (Proverbs 11:24). While the opposite of this verse is in Job 3:25, "For what I **fear** *comes* upon me, and what I dread befalls me." "The worst of my fears has come true, what I've dreaded most has happened." Message Bible.

When we are afraid that we will not have enough, we fear, then we withhold what is justly due for us to prosper (by giving to our enemies *more* than they asked for or demand from us). This withholding results "in want"—so that the fear of not having enough and the dread of being short on funds befalls us! This is the horribly vicious and endless cycle that so many Christians live and what the world "witnesses." And the truth is that this futility can only be broken by receiving all the love that the Lord has for each of us as we become His bride, so that we can trust Him enough to walk out what He has told us, "But I say to you . . ." "give and it shall be given, pressed down and overflowing." Who of us doesn't want to receive *overflowing* blessings?!? We all do, but it takes *giving* when it's difficult to do, and giving to whomever we don't believe *deserves* it.

If giving is something that you have found hard to do, the source is that you still do not have enough of Him. What you need is not more money, but more of Him who loves you in such a way as you really truly feel like His bride! When we seek the Lord and His love wholeheartedly and want, yearn for and focus on only Him, He promises that, "all these things will be **added** to you" (Matthew 6:33). No longer will things or other people matter in your life. It's really true. Once you have enough of Him, you'll want more and more of Him—not things, or money or other people. You won't want attention nor need companionship. And it's then that you will finally be free to *give* because the love that saved this world will be overflowing in your life! You then no longer need or want things, money or people—then all of these blessing will be "pressed down and overflowing" to the point that anyone who comes close to you will be drenched by His blessings too.

This is the secret of life—He gave.

"For **God so** *loved* the world, that He ***gave*** His only begotten Son, that whoever believes in Him shall not perish, but have eternal life" (John 3:16).

—————— Chapter 3 ——————

The Wave of Adversity

Do not resist an evil person . . .
—Matthew 5:38

In the last chapter I shared briefly, explaining that riding the wave of adversity means that you go **with** the flow, never opposing evil that's coming against you. And how it was actually Jesus Himself who explained how we are to react when people tell you to do something, and that He made sure you knew it was He Who said it, *"But **I** say to you . . ."* "But I say to you, do not resist an evil person; but whoever slaps you on your right cheek, turn the other to him also. If anyone wants to sue you and take your shirt, let him have your coat also. Whoever forces you to go one mile, go with him two. Give to him who asks of you, and do not turn away from him who wants to borrow from you" (Matthew 5:39-42).

I'd also confessed that I made sure never to stand close enough to anyone who'd once "slapped" me through their words or actions, and if forced to see them, I'd once made sure to stand back emotionally. There is no doubt that just being willing to stay close to those who've been unkind is difficult, but I'm sure we can all agree that to **do** *more* or **give** *more* than what this same person asked or demanded is nearly impossible to do. But that's when all those "nothing is impossible" verses come in handy. Let's read them:

"And looking at them Jesus said to them, 'With people this is impossible, but *with* God all things are possible'" (Matthew 19:26).

"Looking at them, Jesus said, 'With people it is impossible, but not *with* God; for all things are possible with God" (Mark 10:27).

"For nothing will be impossible *with* God" (Luke 1:37).

"But He said, 'The things that are impossible with people are possible *with* God'" (Luke 18:27).

What makes everything *possible* is when God sent us His Son, to love us in the manner in which a woman could be made to feel truly loved—this is what makes all things possible for us to do. If we fall short of really having enough of His love, it will keep us from not even being able to consider venturing into the principle of riding the wave of adversity. And without any of His love, women will either foolishly fight adversity, only to be hurt even more deeply, or she will run from it.

What I also did my best to expound upon in the last chapter, was what changed me. Once again it was simply finding my abundant life—getting everything I needed **directly** from God like wisdom, and **directly** from the Lord, like the love that I desperately needed.

So can we finally all agree that giving is an incredibly powerful act, but it becomes even more powerful when it is demanded, stolen, or asked for unkindly? True, you may think it's powerfully painful, but the truth is, once you have enough of His love to ponder this principle, you'll begin to realize that adversity, as I understand it now, is actually the fuel we need, or like watering the seed that will bring about a bountiful harvest—the many promises we've been waiting for Him to give us. You may think it's easy for me to say, but like you, I've lived through many difficulties in my life, but now I'm finally able to benefit from them.

My many years of ministry first began the same way Erin's did when my husband also left me, and going through it, like many of you, He lead me to RMI and her teachings. The Lord then began to teach me many of His principles for living my life abundantly, getting me ready for what was up ahead in my life. Each principle, as I walked it out, changed my life significantly. Yet, I have to say that this brand new principle has to be one of the most powerful, which is also a principle that I never, ever, remember hearing from a pulpit or reading in a Christian book. And though Erin may have mentioned it somewhere in her books, I believe she did, I never remember grasping this truth before.

Now, since my living it, to me, this has to be the single most amazing principle to live by which, I promise, will change your life forever. And the reason I believe this, is because this very principle was the way that Jesus lived His life. A life surrounded by adversity, hatred, misunderstanding, betrayal, rejection, and every other evil that made up His very short life while here on earth.

The foundation of this principle is simply this—do **not** resist evil.

There is nothing so natural, so ingrained into our very being, than to do just the opposite. We can't help but resist evil that's being done to us. As a matter of fact, the Christian is taught from the very beginning of his Christian walk to resist and fight every evil and every evil person who tries to come against him or gets in his way. Some may cite these two verses to prove this to be true:

"Submit therefore to God, **resist the devil** and he will flee from you" (James 4:7).

"For we **wrestle not** against **flesh** and blood, but against principalities, against powers, against the rulers of the darkness of this world, against spiritual wickedness in high places" (Ephesians 6:12, KJV).

Though we do see this principle of resisting and wrestling in Scripture, nevertheless this is talking about resisting **us** from doing evil—not resisting evil being done **to** us. There is a vast difference between resisting the devil who is tempting you to do something evil, and also wrestling against principalities and the spiritual wickedness that tries to feed our flesh. So when I say to not resist evil, once again, it's any evil being done TO us.

Needing His Spirit

One principle I know I did learn from Erin was the way we can easily measure if something is from the Lord or not. Somewhere she taught that if we can do something on our own, we're working in the flesh. While the opposite is also true: if we need the help of the Holy Spirit, it means it's clearly from Him.

May I also confess that fighting against evil used to come naturally to me as well (or running from it). Therefore, couldn't we very well conclude that if something was coming "naturally" to me, then it's probable that it was my own flesh that was fighting or running? Also true is that what changed was me knowing that to no longer feel the need to fight or flee was due to what His love did to change me.

Yet maybe even more interesting, an even more powerful and completely overlooked truth, is the fact that Jesus lived His life in order that we, especially we women, could follow His example and were actually "called" to do so.

"For you have been **called** for this purpose, since Christ also suffered for you, leaving you an example for you to follow in His steps . . . and while being reviled, **He did not revile in return;** while suffering, **He uttered no threats,** but kept entrusting Himself to Him (God) who judges righteously" (1 Peter 2:21-23). And the reason I said "especially women" is because immediately following this section in First Peter 2 is when women, specifically, are told how to submit to a husband who is disobedient to the word or in rebellion. "*In the same way*, you wives, be submissive to your own husbands, so that if any of them are disobedient to the word, they may be won without a word by the behavior of their wives, as they observe your chaste and respectful behavior" (1 Peter 3:1–2). Once again, if there is any relationship that would be difficult to "in the same way" suffer, not revile in return even though suffering, and not uttering threats (of leaving or in today's world, calling the police), it is in the relationship with a husband who we trusted to love us, right? And let me say this too, once you're able to do it in the husband/wife relationship, as long as you remain as close to Him and continue doing the same thing in all your other relationships and situations, it actually feels like a "piece of cake" or "walk in the park." Oh, but wait, a thought just flew across my mind.

Frantic and Desperate

There are countless women today, and the numbers are growing, who are more than willing to suffer like this, giving more, turning the other cheek again and again and again. But sadly their motivation is entirely different than what I'm talking about here in this chapter. The horribly damaged woman of today puts herself in a whirlwind of pain, giving over and over and over, more than is asked, hoping that by doing so she will gain the love she is frantic and desperate for! Some dear women are so used to living this way that she seems to be drawn to this same sort of man, again and again and again.

You may not care enough to stop this cycle for your own sake, but will you stop to ponder long enough to stop this vicious cycle for the sake of your daughter, or your sister, or your niece or coworker, aunt or cousin? Until we are willing and brave enough to break free and find the Love that can move the highest mountains of pain and hurt and humiliation and emotional scars, we have no hope to offer anyone. Please don't keep reading this chapter until you first stop to really grasp how important it is for you to learn to live this way. And then being willing to offer this hope, by sharing your own failures and hurts, so when the next woman in pain and fear who is frantic for love comes along, she then learns the truth. Help her to finally learn the depths of His love for her and what that would mean to her life.

Willingly Taken to the Cleaners

Now for an example of how He was helping me grasp this principle by sharing my own personal experience about what happened from the onset of the church-wide announcement from my ex-husband when he told everyone from the pulpit that he was divorcing me. Without really understanding this principle at the time, the Lord led me to not resist evil, not to defend myself when dozens of concerned or outraged members demanded I explain myself. Whether it was my ex-husband stating his demands for the divorce or the insults and accusation of church members, some having been close friends, due to His love alone—I instead was able to enthusiastically agree with what was said, using His example of not opening my mouth, like my Husband who "kept entrusting Himself to Him (God) who judges righteously."

Many of the details of what He brought me through are in the *Facing Divorce* book that RMI offers as one of their many free resources, so I won't go into details. (If you missed reading this book, please go to their website listed at the back of this book.) My point is that all throughout those early days in the very beginning of me finding the abundant life, He was leading me to walk out the principle of not resisting evil. Again, beginning with my ex-husband telling me privately, then telling my children, and then going as far as to announce it on Sunday, the day he turned in his resignation.

Yet, I'm not alone in being taken through adversity—yes, it's how the Lord not only taught just me, but also Erin, who was willing to share all the many principles that we each found (and are continuing to find) in the RMI resources. And if you've been in her resources as long as I have, you'll see there is one common golden thread that ties them all together! How all joy happens through our intimacy with Him and seeking the Lord to help us through each of our difficult situations. This is the only way we too will learn principles that will dramatically change each of our lives and help change the lives of others! Hence this principle can't be accomplished by merely reading about it, but by walking *through* it, after experiencing His love to this degree.

In my own life, from the moment that I first heard my husband announce that he was divorcing me, I found that it didn't take too much on my part to *not* resist evil that was coming against me. Then as the year wore on, it seemed to get easier and easier. Over the years, I've surmised that it must be that previous year (my hardest year ever) when it started. That year served to kill whatever flesh I had left—or so it seemed. Then with my flesh dead, I was able to absorb even more of His love. I also discovered that my flesh is clearly attached directly into the depths of my heart where my children and their well-being are concerned. I know that all of you who are mothers can easily identify when I say that when it comes to our children, there seems to be something built in that instinctively causes us to fight for them.

Yet, even then, God has a way of aligning our hearts with His when He reminds us what it took for *us* to know and experience Him—it was in the midst of adversity wasn't it? So for me, the most important thing in my life (next to my intimacy with my Beloved Lord) is to see each of my children walking a powerful and intimate relationship with the Lord themselves. Which means that they too will need to walk a life filled with adversity in order to experience Him. Yes, like Erin, "I have no greater joy than this, to hear of my children walking in Truth" (3 John 1:4).

So if I am going to let adversity strike not just me, but my children, without my being tempted to step in between them or even cushioning the blow done to them, then I must make sure to give them and teach them the principles and be the example for them to see how. To help my children *through,* just as I do for women I meet in my church or in my ministering, I need to know, live and share this principle. Though I know I must be exaggerating, but often it feels as if there is at least one new attack each week coming at my children, pounding away at the very foundation of their lives, which for children is the area of **safety**. Children (and women) need to know that they are safe and that no harm is going to come against them to cause them pain. This is the security that children need to grow, and women need in order to flourish.

We've each heard about the effects on many television talk shows when they delve into how things that happen in a child's past are sure to stunt or inhibit the natural maturity process and scar them for life. We are told how these children are left "emotionally retarded" and are "scarred" adults who are full of problems and struggles that find their way into every facet of their adult lives. Some of us *are* these adults. So how can we possible help our children, or help ourselves as wounded adults, when it seems that the entire world is just one giant adversity coming against us with no relief?

By believing what He told us, "I have told you these things, so that in Me you may have peace. In this world **you *will* have trouble.** But take heart! I have ***overcome*** the world" (John 16:33). Jesus was able to overcome the world, I believe, through this one principle that is never taught, much less walked out by today's Christian. It is what He taught us from the beginning of His ministry:

Once again, give, and listen when He says, "*I say to you,* **do not resist an evil person;** but whoever slaps you on your right cheek, turn the other to him also. If anyone wants to sue you and take your shirt, let him have your coat also. Whoever forces you to go one mile, go with him two" (Matthew 5:38–40).

The very first portion states it clearly, read it again—*do not resist.*

Let's think about this for a moment. What if Jesus had *resisted* His death on the cross, where would we be? Remember how Peter instinctively resisted (by cutting off the guard's ear) and was rebuked by Jesus (who healed the man's ear). Peter also lied. He then ran and hid (much like many of us do) when adversity came against him, even though he was an eye witness to Jesus and His example of not resisting evil. Yet, Jesus knew that to *resist* is natural; therefore, He explained **up front** how He was going to live (by not resisting) and then showed the ultimate proof of the power of this principle by riding the wave of adversity all the way to the cross.

Due to Him wanting more for me, I have been called to learn, live and teach this principle. Only then could I now come to see in my own life, and also by taking a closer look at the life of Jesus, that instead of resisting, we can actually **use** the adversity as a smooth and easy ride that leads us right to the blessings, as well as giving us an elevated platform that we can use to give God the glory He deserves and stand tall to share His love with others!

An Analogy

One day while flying (somewhere), the Lord showed me an analogy of this principle of not resisting evil like a surfer who rides "a wave of adversity" to shore. This was easy for me to understand since I am a California girl and grew up body surfing. So since many of you may be landlocked, I will do my best to help you to understand this principle. This analogy has not only helped me, but it has helped my children understand and work this principle into their lives.

The Lord showed me a group of people who come to the ocean but they simply sit on the safe sand far from getting into the foreboding waves. I remember these as the tourists who came fully clothed and never really intending to swim. Then I saw another group who stood with their feet in the white waters that moved back and forth with the tide. I remembered as a little girl that women would often stand with their pant legs rolled up and talk as they enjoyed just enough, but not too much, of the ocean. When I would stand next to them, I found that if I just stood still the washing of the waves back and forth would often cause my feet to become buried until I couldn't easily move. Interesting.

Next, He showed me the somewhat brave who would venture out a bit further into the waves. One wave after another would hit and often knock them down, since they were not up higher on the sand like the ladies, nor were they out far enough in the water where the waves would swell but not crash right on top of them. Though they thought they were safer closer to shore, rather than moving out deeper, they were, in fact, directly in the path of the weight of each wave, which resulted in them getting knocked down until they were worn out. Some of these braver souls would watch, as other swimmers would dive just beneath the waves seconds before crashing. Yet, even these better, braver swimmers would soon tire and have to return to the shore to rest and recover after diving through enough waves.

Finally, there were those eager souls who had learned the secret to these adverse waves. These swimmers would swim out to where it was deep, then turn to watch for the big waves, and rather than fighting against it, they would confidently then turn and paddle towards shore, choosing to work *with* the wave and use its fury to ride it to its destination. They were actually "riding the wave of adversity" and taking full advantage of its power, using its anger for their good.

The Lord didn't stop His allegory there. I envisioned further down the coast where there was an area restricted, no swimmers allowed, where only the surfers with their surfboards were allowed to ride the largest waves —and they were not alone. Sitting up on the shore were the many spectators who gathered to watch or stand in awe. These, the Lord showed me, were those saints who used the waves of adversity as a platform to show God's greatness. Instead of dreading the largest waves, they would actually look for them in great anticipation.

This is what the Lord wanted me to begin doing and what I want to encourage you to look forward to in your own life.

Platform to Show His Greatness

While traveling and speaking to women on an individual basis or before a large church, or anywhere in between, I found myself sharing several testimonies with them, though I hadn't planned to. The larger the wave of adversity that I shared that I had ridden on, the greater their excitement when I shared it. The two waves of adversity that ultimately got the greatest ooohs and ahhhs, were the ones that many Christians had actually criticized and mocked me for—as being foolish or even being contrary to the word of God. One was when I paid for my ex-husband's honeymoon and also when I spoke to my ex-husband (after his engagement was announced) and encouraged him to be good and patient with his new, soon-to-be wife. The women in Africa especially got excited about those two testimonies since they were quite clear (even the director of a huge worldwide ministry that spreads over all the nations of Africa), and told me that if it were *their* husband they wouldn't pay for a honeymoon or encourage him to be nice to that other woman, but would instead find something big and "deadly" to beat him (and the other woman) with!

Yet, those waves of adversity are the very ones that forced these same Christians to have to think about their own lives and how they lived, and what impact it's made on the lost souls of this world. What the world "witnesses" tells many different stories of His life and His love or speaks contrary to it. Nevertheless, it wasn't the women (or men) in the church that I was most excited to share my "riding the wave of adversities" stories with. It was when I was blessed to share them with strangers, who then became interested in knowing "that God" whom they had never heard of. What the Lord was showing me was that these were the kind of waves that I need to begin watching for and not dreading, and like the surfers on their boards, I need to actually be looking for and be excited to ride!

Preparing Us

Of course, to learn any new principle, it will always need the right circumstances to apply them; thankfully, these are coming regularly right now in my life and maybe in your life too. There is always a swell of a wave in the horizon, recently, in regard to the custody of my youngest children. The next one will reach me within 24 hours when my ex-husband arrives for an "unscheduled visit" that my children are sure will mean another adverse, possibly, huge wave.

Yet, custody is not the only continual waves that are hitting me, because back there in the ocean of adversities, I can clearly see a tsunami in regard to my finances. Like many surfers, when you see the big ones, you are both a tad scared while at the same time, a bit excited. Will I be able to hang on? Will I be able to maneuver along it gracefully knowing that so many are watching? Or, will I instead chicken out and paddle toward the swelling wave (taking matters into my own hands) and miss the platform to glorify God and shout about the Lord's Love?

To gain courage, my thoughts always seem to rewind back to each of the waves that the Lord has brought me through thus far, which helps me to gain the courage that I will need to "go for it." At the same time, being human, I fight the thoughts that try to creep into my mind with the many "what if" scenarios that envision me, such as "wiping out"—which is a surfer term that I don't think I need to explain. However, just a quick walk through the marked promises in my Bible, or even a brief moment of intimacy with the Lord, and those visions are replaced with the trust that I am going to need. For me to give God the glory that He deserves once again, and to really show the Love that is there for each woman from her Husband who died to give her His abundant life here on earth, I need to always remember that this is all about Him and nothing at all about me.

The platform that He has built just for you and me is for the very purpose that we will inherit a blessing (and these are what I am gathering to leave as an inheritance for my children). These "waves of adversity" are created to get the attention of the unbeliever and make him want to know Jesus personally, while at the same time, used to motivate the common Christian to live a life hidden in and cultivated in deep intimacy with Him.

Now, Precious reader and dear friend, get excited, as you get ready to ride the next wave that is headed your way.

Chapter 4

When Do I Give Up?

"My yoke is easy and
My burden is light"
—Matthew 11:30

As a Christian, you and I will each face times in our lives when all we want to do is give up. No great man or woman who we've read about, no matter how noble, has not experienced the feelings or thoughts of quitting—not one. Even Jesus, on His knees, with blood dripping from His brow asked God if there was "another way" other than the cross when He prayed that night in Gethsemane. It is natural, and even expected to have these feelings.

The difference between those who are later considered "great," versus those who never make it into the pages we Christians read for encouragement, is what that person does with the thought or feeling of quitting. Those who may have been called to greatness, those whom we never hear from again are the ones who act on those thoughts and feelings—turning back. Yet, those who go on, like Jesus, are those who rely on Someone and something greater to carry them through. LOVE. "For God so **loved** the world..." (John 3:16).

The man who wrote most of the New Testament, the apostle Paul, had a lot to say about giving up. He said, finally, "I have fought the good fight, I have finished the course, I have kept the faith, in the future there is laid up for me the crown of righteousness, which the Lord, the righteous Judge, will award to me on that day; and not only to me, but also to all who have loved His appearing" (2 Timothy 4:7-8).

Did this man, Paul, have to endure and pass through very much in order to be such a help to us? One day, while having to defend himself to the Corinthians, he said this, "I speak as if insane—I more so; in far more labors, in far more imprisonments, beaten times without number, often in danger of death. Five times I received from the Jews thirty-nine lashes. Three times I was beaten with rods, once I was stoned, three times I was shipwrecked, a night and a day I have spent in the deep.

"I have been on frequent journeys, in dangers from rivers, dangers from robbers, dangers from my countrymen, dangers from the Gentiles, dangers in the city, dangers in the wilderness, dangers on the sea, dangers among false brethren; I have been in labor and hardship, through many sleepless nights, in hunger and thirst, often without food, in cold and exposure.

"Apart from such external things, there is the daily pressure on me of concern for all the churches. Who is weak without my being weak?" (2 Corinthians 11:23–29).

Most of us cringe when we think of enduring such hardship in order to help others with our testimony. When it comes right down to it, unless *we* get something out of it, most of us will simply give up and turn back. To be honest with you, what I "used to" hope to get out of my adversities along my journey was a verse that many Christian leaders hang onto when they want to hear Jesus tell them, "Well done, good and faithful servant!" (Matthew 25:21). Yet, even that thought no longer motivates me now—not winning, not even the prize that the Apostle Paul uses to motivate you and me (and I have always been a very competitive person). Part of the reason is that I would prefer my Husband be Who greets me, *not* as His "good and faithful servant" but embracing me in the way I imagine my Bridegroom doing— grabbing hold and swinging me around the clouds upon our meeting when I leave this earth.

Paul also said, "I do all things for the sake of the gospel, so that I may become a fellow partaker of it. Do you not know that those who run in a race all run, but only one *receives the prize*? Run in such a way that you may **win.** Everyone who competes in the games exercises self-control in all things. They then do it to receive a perishable wreath, but we an imperishable" (1 Corinthians 9:23-25).

Once again, Paul tries to motivate you and me while writing to the Philippians, "Therefore, since we have so great a cloud of **witnesses** surrounding us [remember this literally means the people in your life who "witness" and watch how you live your life differently], let us also lay aside every encumbrance and the sin which so easily entangles us, and let us run with endurance the race that is set before us, **fixing our eyes on Jesus**, the author and perfecter of faith, who for the joy set before Him endured the cross, *despising* **the shame**, and has sat down at the right hand of the throne of God. For consider Him who has endured such hostility by sinners against Himself, so that you will not grow weary and lose heart" (Hebrews 12:1-3).

Though many of you have read this verse in Hebrews, I found another version that seemed to fit just a bit better this morning in *The Message Bible*.

"Do you see what this means—all these pioneers who blazed the way, all these veterans cheering us on? It means we'd better get on with it. Strip down, start running—and never quit! No extra spiritual fat, no parasitic sins. Keep your eyes on Jesus, who both began and finished this race we're in. Study how He did it. Because He never lost sight of where He was headed—that exhilarating finish in and with God—He could put up with anything along the way: Cross, shame, whatever. And now He's there, in the place of honor, right alongside God. When you find yourselves flagging in your faith, go over that story again, item by item, that long litany of hostility he plowed through. That will shoot adrenaline into your souls!" (Hebrews 12:1-3 Message).

Again, though I love imagining sitting alongside God, I do so imagining sitting with my Husband, by His side. As a woman, we are born and created to desire this kind of love, not the selfish, self-centered, self-serving love of the human race—light-years and plans beyond what most could imagine.

"Now glory be to God, who by his mighty power at work within us is able to do far more than we would ever dare to ask or even dream of—infinitely beyond our highest prayers, desires, thoughts, or hopes" (Ephesians 3:20 TLB).

"God can do anything, you know—far more than you could ever imagine or guess or request in your wildest dreams!" (Ephesians 3:20 Message).

Analogy of a Full Moon Witness

Looking at the full moon outside my window, I found myself talking to the Lord like I always do. Being Sunday, I forced myself to stay off my computer to take the much needed day of rest with Him. What I found myself saying was that the *full* moon is like us when we face Him our Sun, His Son, when the world is not blocking or getting in the way of how we live our lives. The beauty, and amazing part, of how God created this universe, is that even if only a sliver of His light shines on our lives, the rest blocked by the many things of this world, even then our *crescent* can and does attract those who are gazing at our lives— looking for hope.

Giving Up:
Turning Back vs Turning it Over

So, yes, I actually came to the place where I wanted to give up, but that's when I realized that whatever I had been doing that caused me to become weary, leading to wanting to give up, had been due to me carrying too much of the load—the burdens He needed to be given! Burdens of planning or thinking or anything else I'd been doing that began to weigh on me. Coming to the overwhelming feelings of wanting to give up is showing me and you that we **need** to give up, in order to turn us to turn everything over to the One who's waiting to take those burdens that He **wants** us to give up—No, not to turn back—but in order for us to realize that He's a Gentlemen, a Warrior, a Provider, and anything else we need rather than **us** doing it.

Read what the Lord's saying to you, "Are you tired? Worn out? Burned out on religion [performing good works in order to please others]? Come to me. Get away with Me and you'll recover your life. I'll show you how to take a real rest. Walk with Me and work with Me—watch how I do it. Learn the unforced rhythms of grace. I won't lay anything heavy or ill-fitting on you. Keep company with Me and you'll learn to live freely and lightly" (Matthew 11:29-30 Message).

The Lord wants to and is equipped to carrying the heavy burdens, even the tiny ones that we think we can manage.

So often the burdens I'm experiencing are due to me being *yoked* to other people's desires or demands on me, and probably even more often, it's due to the yoke I've put on myself, desires and demands or perfections, I've put on myself.

Again listen to what He's saying to you, "Take My yoke upon you and learn from Me, for I am gentle and humble in heart, and you will find rest for your souls. For My yoke is easy and My burden is light" (Matthew 11:29-30). HIS yoke is always light and easy. So when we feel like giving up, give up that burdensome yoke and exchange it for His—light and easy—where we will find rest for our very souls.

The reason He led me to write this chapter, I believe, is because this morning I received another letter from a woman who wrote to let me know she's quitting. I get so many letters of women quitting, though I believe there are many more who quit and never write to me or RMI.

So, for all of you who want to quit, give up, throw in the towel, find an easier path, please DO. But rather than turning back to your old life or something the world will gladly offer you (leading to more pain), sit down where you are OR better yet, run to and fling yourself into His waiting arms. Let Him hold you tightly, assuring you that everything that has made you worn out isn't His yoke at all.

"The Lord is my Shepherd, I shall not want. He makes me lie down in green pastures; He leads me beside quiet waters. He restores my soul" (Psalm 23: 1-3). Then during your time of laying down in those cushy green pastures, next to the still waters, together you can sort out all that you need to give to Him.

It was just two days ago that all I could think about all day long was that all of this, all that I have gone through and am going through (and wow, things have been very tough lately and seem to get tougher every day), is for just one reason—to know Him, to yoke myself to Him and to allow all of this as His way of showing me how to live my life differently. Living it abundantly. There is no other way around learning this truth.

Nothing else matters, but in knowing Him personally and living your life yoked to Him—nothing in my life, nothing in your life (not even if this is **not** how you *feel* or how you *think*).

For those who want to hear praise "well done" remember, a trophy gets dusty, praise ceases to feel the same, prestige and fame come with a price. That's why again it's important that we understand that there was only one thing that motivated those whom we now look to for encouragement, those individuals who one day became great—it was because through everything, they came to know Him.

As Paul said, paraphrased by the Message Bible, "The very credentials these people are waving around as something special, I'm tearing up and throwing out with the trash—along with everything else I used to take credit for. And why? Because of Christ. Yes, all the things I once thought were so important are gone from my life. Compared to the high privilege of **knowing** Christ Jesus as my Master [**my Lover**], firsthand, everything I once thought I had going for me is insignificant—dog dung. I've dumped it all in the trash so that I could *embrace* Christ and **be embraced by Him**" (Philippians 3:7-9 Message).

Let me close by assuring you of this one fact I've learned Living the Abundant Life, "My beloved is mine, and I am His . . . When I found Him whom my soul loves; I held on to Him and would not let him go . . . **For I am [wonderfully] lovesick**" (Song of Solomon 3:2–4; 5:8).

Chapter 5

Small as a Man's Fist

After the seventh time the servant replied,
"I see a small cloud coming this way.
But it's no bigger than a fist."
—1 Kings 18:44, CEV

The opening verse is referring to the faith of Elijah, the prophet, and has always been one of my favorite verses due to its principle that I love to embrace. As a matter of fact, it is one of the reasons that Erin began posting praise reports on the RMI site, how she said, sharing praise reports got started. Back when these started, she announced that she wanted them to teach the ministry members to look for their "very small cloud" that would announce, in faith, that their miracle was on its way. Hearing this, I began submitting praise reports regularly, announcing each time the Lord would do something in my life so that other women could get excited, no matter how small the cloud.

If you have also read her *Restore Your Marriage* book, then you've read the many verses in it that are on faith. Just to refresh all of our minds, let me list just a few of my favorites:

"And Jesus answered and said to them, 'Truly I say to you, if you have **faith,** and do not doubt, you shall not only do what was done . . . but even if you say to this mountain, "Be taken up and cast into the sea," it shall happen'" (Matthew 21:21). No matter how impossible.

"So **faith** comes from *hearing*, and *hearing* by the Word of Christ" (Romans 10:17). Again building each other's faith by hearing about that impossibility He's doing in your life, no matter how small.

Lastly, probably my two absolute favorites being: "Now **faith** is the assurance of things ***hoped*** for, the conviction of things ***not* seen**" (Hebrews 11:1). "And without **faith** it is impossible to please God . . ." (Hebrews 11:6).

Yet, in lieu of the principle for this chapter, it is this next verse that probably is the most important regarding our faith: "In this you greatly rejoice, even though for a little while, if necessary, you have been distressed by various trials, that the *proof of your faith,* being more precious than gold (which is perishable) even though tested by fire, may be found to result in praise, glory and honor" (1 Peter 1:6–7).

The proof of Elijah's faith was more precious than gold to God since its result was praise, glory, and honor to Him. God doesn't need our money, since all the gold and silver (and everything in and on the earth) are His anyway. God only asks for us to tithe it, and then also bless others with it as an offering, in order to open up the windows of heaven over us. Even in our giving, He is peeking into our very souls to see our faith. Do we trust Him or not?

Funny that finances just happened to be the first example that came to mind when speaking about faith, because this is really what I want to share with you. This week, I received a small cloud in the mail, money that was no bigger than a man's fist. So just as Elijah was totally and completely confident that just seeing that tiny cloud meant that the rain was about to ***pour*** over his life, so too, am I totally confident that my showers (a torrential rain) is about to hit in my finances. Confident is actually defined as "certain of having the ability, judgment, and resources needed to succeed." Yes, Lord.

So, Wow—this pretty much sums up exactly what I want to say; I have the confidence in God that He has the ability, judgment, *and* of course, the resources needed to help me succeed. My confidence is not in myself—by no means! As a matter of fact, I know that I do not have the ability, judgment, nor the resources needed to succeed in my new position as a single mother of so many children, and I also don't have the ability, judgment, or resources to provide for them myself—which is why I watch for the cloud indicating the downpour is coming.

"Now Elijah said to Ahab, 'Go up, eat and drink; for there is the **sound of the roar** of a **heavy shower**.' So Ahab went up to eat and drink. But Elijah went up to the top of Carmel; and he crouched down on the earth and put his face between his knees. He said to his servant, "Go up now, look toward the sea." So he went up and looked and said, "There is nothing." And he said, "Go back" **seven times.** It came about at the *seventh* time, that he said, "Behold, a cloud as small as a man's hand is coming up from the sea." And he said, 'Go up, say to Ahab, 'Prepare your chariot and go down, so that the heavy shower does not stop you.'' In a little while the sky grew black with clouds and wind, and there was a heavy shower" (1 Kings 18:41-45).

This story of Elijah began with God causing a drought that was over Samaria where he lived. And this drought was brought about by God in order to **put** Elijah *in the position* of bringing Him glory (and to destroy evil in their land). It is one of my absolute favorite stories in the Bible for many reasons. First it reminds me that each situation we find ourselves in, God sets us up, putting us in the position to show His power and to elevate us. And what makes me want to shout and dance is in witnessing the faith a man who saw only a tiny little cloud, when he really *needed* and was *anticipating* a torrential downpour, who, just by seeing the tiny cloud caused him to move into action. How awesome!!

Notice even before it could be heard, Elijah said there IS a sound of a heavy shower. This reminds me of this next verse I memorized early on in my journey that I said was one of my favorites, "So then faith comes by *hearing*, and hearing by the word of God." What he heard was God's word saying that we could trust Him to this extent. Though Elijah sent his servant to eat and drink, he instead remained in communion with God. In the Message bible it says he, "bowed deeply in prayer" that I too imagine him doing or maybe he bowed down to simply listen.

Of course, the best part is how Elijah continued, a full 7 times, to tell his servant to go look— KNOWING the clouds would come! And again, it wasn't that his servant came running back shouting that he saw a storm on the horizon or blowing their way. All he said he saw was a tiny cloud no bigger than the size of a man's fist! So this means that it's not when you receive that big check you were hoping for, but something so small and insignificant that it may not even pay one of your overdue bills. Or, in the case of being healed, it's not that you can get up and walk, it's that you can feel just the slightest sensation in one of your feet.

Additional proof of his faith is that Elijah didn't wait to send his servant until more rainclouds formed, but with just this tiny cloud he urges him to go right away, warning him not to wait, lest he be caught in the downpour so it wouldn't prevent him from letting everyone know the rains were coming!!

How's that for exciting? And, if you really want to get excited, just read 1 Kings 18 in its entirety. No, better yet, start back with 1 Kings 17, because it shows us something else about God—He builds our faith to the point that we, too, will see just the small cloud for us to also act with total belief.

Knowing how Elijah's faith blesses me, I can only imagine how it blessed God when there are only a small few of all humanity who've trusted Him to that level—and I want to be one of them. How about you? What's your level of faith these days? Funny how we Christians are. We claim we want a powerful testimony, but we don't want to go through the horribly difficult situations and crises that produce those kind of testimonies—the ones that change lives as they witness our faith and peace in the midst of them. Never relying on ourselves or others to help, but simply waiting, listening and trusting that He will do what He promised.

Yet, as with all things, it takes the Lord and His love to change us to the degree we can exercise this kind of faith—and often, it means He'll be the One Who carries us—carries us *through* those crises that rock our world. I know. Honestly, it's during the "carrying me" crises that we are really changed the most dramatically. My guess is that when He carries us, we are resting so very close to His heart. This alone should help us never to fear what terrible catastrophes might be up ahead for us to walk *through*. And if we're in His loving arms, even burying our faces deeply into His chest, we know He can bring us through or over anything, right? Just mentioning this to you has brought me great peace and joy in the midst of my current situation. I hope it has done the same for you too!

So before we move to the next chapter, let's end this one by reading another of my favorite verses and one that I recently used when it appeared that there was no hope.

"Though the fig tree should not blossom and there be no fruit on the vines, Though the yield of the olive should fail and the fields produce no food, Though the flock should be cut off from the fold and there be no cattle in the stalls, **YET** I will exult in the Lord, I will rejoice in the God of my salvation. The Lord God is my strength, and He has made my feet like hinds' feet, and makes me walk on my high places" (Habakkuk 3:17-19).

Amplified: "**Yet** I will [**choose** to] rejoice in the Lord; I will [*choose* to] shout in exultation in the [victorious] God of my salvation! The Lord God is my strength [my source of courage, my invincible army]; He has made my feet [steady and sure] like hinds' feet and makes me walk [forward with spiritual confidence] on my high places [of challenge and responsibility]."

The Voice: "**Even if** the fig tree does not blossom and there are no grapes on the vines, If the olive trees fail to give fruit and the fields produce no food, If the flocks die far from the fold and there are no cattle in the stalls; Then I will **still** rejoice in the Eternal! **I will** rejoice in the God who saves me! The Eternal Lord is my strength! He has made my feet like the feet of a deer; He allows me to walk on high places."

If you struggle with praising God with total and complete faith in the MIDST of crises, then I'd suggest purchasing or going to your local library to get the book *Prison to Praise* by Merlin R. Carothers. And if you're concerned that the Lord will allow the fires of your life get too hot for you to handle, be sure you read October 29 in the Streams in the Desert devotional, which opens with the verse, "He will sit as a refiner and purifier of silver" (Malachi 3:3) and its poem ends with,

So He waited there with a watchful eye,
With a love that is strong and sure,
And His gold did not suffer a bit more heat,
Than was needed to make it pure.

Chapter 6

That Amazing Grace

The **amazing grace** of the Master, Jesus Christ,
the extravagant love of God,
the intimate friendship of the Holy Spirit,
be with all of you.
—2 Corinthians 13:14 MSG

This morning my daughter thought that I had the air conditioning on in the car (when it was freezing outside), and asked if I was having one of my hot flashes. I told her no, but I had had a few earlier in the morning.

Though I had never planned to discuss something so personal with my children, surprisingly, they were made aware of my latest "condition" from an old television sitcom that they were watching during lunch one afternoon. Point blank one of my older sons turned to me (the one who has no filters) asking me, since I was "about that age; wasn't I?" was I "going through the change of life?" I had to confess that, yes, I was, though as I said, I had never planned to say anything to anyone.

Very personal topics are not only openly discussed on television, but also in public and all throughout the workplace. Women are speaking indiscriminately, even reacting to hot flashes indiscreetly, and discussing every other thing that plagues a woman's life, very openly. Apart from wanting to simply remain quiet about what I'm going through, discussing it only with my Husband, my question is "Where is the grace?" grace to cover us and provide concealment for things that should be allowed to remain private. Whether I am going through loss in my life, a horrendous crisis, a hot flash or night sweats, or feeling as if I am on an emotional rollercoaster, I want desperately to do it gracefully and accept it graciously from the Lord without drawing attention to myself. It's not because I'm shy, it's because I want my life to have the title of Him, not me, as a witness. "Ye are our epistles written in our hearts, known and read of all men" (2 Corinthians 3:2 KJV) "You are our letter, written in our hearts, known and read by all men."

Years ago, I am sure because of my immaturity before beginning my restoration journey, I didn't at all handle difficult situations well. I stupidly believed I had to react; and have since learned, such is not the case. Even though I may never have been as "bad" as I often witness in other women, nevertheless, each time I did *give into* my feelings, I was left feeling even **worse** for having *reacted*. Most of us have heard from psychologists (who know nothing, since they usually tell us the opposite of what God says in the Bible) that we have to let it out like a tea kettle. Did you know that this theory was proven wrong years ago, but it is still widely accepted as truth?

The truth is that when we do let things out, we usually feel worse and are also left with other people's reactions and responses to deal with on top of our own. True, we may feel good initially, but these good feelings don't last, not to mention the domino effect that has been set in motion; the consequences of having to deal with the feelings of the other person(s) we told. Whether the others react in anger or are hurt or confused, now they are added to the mix. In my own life, when I "let it out" and *reacted*, I realized I was always left feeling worse about my situation, but even more tragic, I also was left with shame, embarrassment, and regrets for having given into my feelings. Interestingly, too, is that each time there was an eyewitness or someone who heard what I said, no matter how many times they told me (sincerely) that it was "okay" or that they "understood," it did not lessen my regrets for having responded stupidly and how so often the good opinion others once had for me, changed forever. And most who said they understood, really didn't or couldn't.

Yet, if we don't "let it out" or "let off steam," won't we soon explode? Actually, no. Not if we keep it to ourselves the way it was intended. Years ago, the Lord showed me that He keeps us in these "pressure situations" to **tenderize** our hearts just like a pressure cooker does! However, in the midst of each pressure, you will not be able to leave the lid on (so to speak) unless you take whatever it is to the Lord and leave the situation with Him. The greatest part of speaking to Him about it is that not only do we get to walk away feeling better, freer, and lighter (as many describe it), but we also walk away with that **amazing *grace*.** It was just this morning that I realized that both the words "*grac*iously" and "*grace*fully" have the root word of that amazing *grace!* Wow, I like that. Bear with me as we discuss more about how a pressure cooker works, so we are able to compare it to what God wants us to do with the pressures in our lives.

A pressure cooker is (our trials are) a sealed pot with a *valve* that **controls** the steam pressure inside (a situation where GOD controls how much He will allow). As the pot/trial heats up, the liquid/His love inside privately forms steam/tears, which raises the pressure in the pot/our lives. This high pressure steam has two major benefits: It raises the boiling point to allow the higher heat to help the food/heart to cook/change *faster*, and as the pressure raises, its forcing liquid/love into the food/heart (in other words, high pressured trials are forcing His love into your heart). The high continuous pressure (of the trial) also helps force liquid/love and moisture/His peace into the food/heart *quickly*, which helps it cook/be completed *faster* and also helps certain foods/hearts, like tough meat/harden hearts, get very **tender** *very quickly*. Also, the flavors/testimonies created in a pressure cooker can be really deep and complex — unlike any other cooking/trial method.

Thanking the Lord just didn't seem like enough when I thought about His amazing grace of understanding what a benefit feeling like a pressure cooker was! The heat or steam I felt I wanted to endure, because like all trials, which are uncomfortable, I know they are doing wonders for my inner being.

What I did to help me not just endure the steam (hot flashes or night sweats) is when I took this to the Lord asking my Husband how to get through these gracefully. What He told me was to embrace them, reminding me of how much I loved being in a hot bath, or Jacuzzi tub or years ago when I went to a gym to sit in a steam room. I had to laugh, of course, why make a scene when I can simply close my eyes and imagine it's really my heavenly Love who's treating me to something special because He loves me?! So the moment I did that, I no longer would dread or worry about when my change of life symptoms would "hit," instead it became a welcomed reminder of His love for me.

By being transparent, discussing something I'd rather not discuss or reveal to anyone, as a friend I hoped that sharing my gratefulness for His amazing grace in just one of my newer trials, it might help you to go to the Lord, asking Him to view your current condition. Whether your condition is physical or situational. And while I've been discussing the hidden truth about how we can begin living our lives gracefully, a comparison popped into mind that I thought might help you. Since remembering the comparison (like God does in His Proverbs, showing one extreme versus the other), it has helped me overcome my tendency to still want to "let it out" or let things be known that should be kept discreetly between "me and my Husband" (I know that is grammatically incorrect, "me" should come after putting the other person first).

Comparison

About 13 years ago, something happened where I lived that became world news. The most amazing thing about this, was that the persons involved were our close friends, members of our church. And the wife was a woman who was in my Wise Woman class; one who had proven to be outspoken.

That day, just like many of you, I watched my television in disbelief, not just about the events that were unfolding, but I became more intrigued by the reaction of the couple as individuals. The husband had learned to be very quiet due to his wife's overreaction to everything. There, on television, I watched as she, once again, made a scene as she had trained herself to do in her life (especially in her marriage). So when the television cameras were live, streaming around the world, the cameras did little to quiet her angry screaming. If anything, seeing she had an audience looked like she began to increase her bad behavior.

Fast forward now about sixteen months later when once again, the news bulletin interrupted television programming, cameras again rolling in our small, once, insignificant small town. This time, I watched my television with even greater disbelief as I saw one of our closest friends, handcuffed while being dragged into police headquarters. Much later, during the trial, I witnessed first-hand this man's wife and couldn't help but draw a comparison between the two wives, the two women I knew personally.

The latter wife, once a pastor's wife, I'd compare to a woman like Jackie Kennedy when her husband, President Kennedy was assassinated. It was due to her very composed demeanor when hundreds of cameras were in her face, along with the screaming reporters, which everyone was a witness to. It showed the world her immeasurable **grace**—beyond what any of us could ever imagine exhibiting if this had happened to us. This woman and her husband had been a close friend, to both my husband (now ex) and I, which is why we remained behind her, supporting her. Not just supporting her emotionally, we also helped them by caring for their children and home (like my boys mowing their lawn), and also choosing to sit behind her at the trial that was televised worldwide. Sadly, we were her *only* support— all, every single one of her other friends, everyone, abandoned her. Why do Christians seem to forget that "a friend loveth at all times" and we are needed the most during the worst of times?

No matter how much I may have helped my friend and her family during this tragic time in her life, which lasted for decades (do any of us want to complain about our situation right now?), she helped me witness true **royalty** first-hand. Yes, royalty. This refined lady exhibited what it means to be a child of the King, whose name is Jesus, and she wore her crown of grace like a princess. I saw her at her best and worse, and whether she was in front of the cameras or if she was behind closed doors with her family, she appeared just the same. In perfect peace.

No one knows if my friend broke down in her prayer closet, only her Lover knows, but what I witnessed forever changed my life. Her example made me want to be like her and all those who've worn their royalty like a crown when facing the worst of times in their lives. I want to be like my friend whom I witnessed up close and behind the scenes, who faced incredible horrific attacks that would grip anyone alive, yet she walked through it fearlessly (or so it appeared) with a gentle and quiet spirit. Truly a princess since I know her true Husband, the Prince of Peace, was always with her, by her side and it showed.

How we react may not change the course of the events we face, but it will diminish the after effects of guilt and shame or ramifications of something that was said, that is added to our already difficult situation—when we give way to our feelings openly. Therefore, the truth is, it won't help us to feel better once we "let it all out," but instead, it will once again be a time when we missed appropriating and tapping into that *amazing grace* that flourishes: the darker the day, the steeper the climb, the harder the fall.

For me, I want to show the world (which starts with my family who are closest to me) that our Husband is real and His grace transcends all difficulties of this life. "These things I have spoken unto you, that in me you might have peace. In the world you will have tribulation: but be of good cheer; I have overcome the world" (John 16:33 KJV). His grace, found in His love, is what helps women "smile at the future" when the future looks like a deep dark hole. It is not that we are brave, not really, but that we know Who holds the future, and we know how His story ends. Let us never forget, too, that it is often the "little foxes that spoil the vine." In other words, it is always the small things that we have to tackle and overcome: things like menopause, marital abandonment, rejection from family, or financial ruin. Only when we conquer our "selves" in the midst of these, can we conquer the big ones that may be up ahead for some of us.

Oh, that amazing grace.

Chapter 7

Believing God for Great Things

For Your righteousness, O God, reaches to the heavens,
You who have done **great things**;
O God, who is like You?
—Psalm 71:19

Just a few minutes ago, I said goodbye to my children as they headed off to church. They really have no idea how much I think about it each week—about not going with them. I really thought that I had come to the place that it no longer mattered, but then to my surprise, just last week the Lord had me go to two services. A well-known evangelist was speaking, someone my older boys said I shouldn't miss. Honestly, I thought I surely would "miss it," but I asked the Lord, and surprising me, He said go. So I went, was blessed, and was given the opportunity to give a substantial amount of money as an offering (the main reason, it seems, for my going to this evening service).

My children, I know, used to question some of the crazy things I did. Most of their questions stemmed from the reputation that their father had painted about me. No doubt it was one of the things that drove him more into the world and the things of it to make him happy. I'm sure, now looking back, it was simply his way of giving him an exit since he'd been planning to reconnect with his high school girlfriend for years, each planning to divorce spouses. At the time, however, I had no idea that he was sharing his thoughts and opinions with the older children, and honestly when I found out I was sure that my reputation with them may never recover. Yet, God has promises for us that far outweigh the negatives of this world.

"In You, O LORD, I have taken refuge; Let me **never be ashamed**; In Your righteousness deliver me" (Psalms 31:1).

"They looked to Him and were radiant, and their faces will **never be ashamed**" (Psalms 34:5).

"In You, O LORD, I have taken refuge; Let me **never be ashamed**" (Psalms 71:1).

"The sons of those who afflicted you will come bowing to you, and all those who despised you will bow themselves at the soles of your feet . . ." (Isaiah 60:14).

"Peter said, 'Behold, we have left our own homes and followed You.' And He said to them, 'Truly I say to you, there is no one who has left house or wife or brothers or parents or children, for the sake of the kingdom of God, who will not receive many times as much at this time and in the age to come, eternal life'" (Luke 18:28–30).

It took the Lord putting me in a very ominous situation within weeks of my divorce, by traveling and financial craziness, to turn the tide, and my reputation with my children also began to turn. As I'd said in earlier chapters, I am just learning how we must expect that we will go through greater, crazier feats when we decided to believe God for great things.

That's what I hope to explain to my children later today at lunch. I want to tell them that all these incredible and crazy things that I am doing now are simply because I am determined to believe God for great things.

Just a week ago, I had the opportunity to share with all of them (some individually), that in myself I haven't a prayer of making it with all that has come against me and continues to do so. It is only the Lord who will be able to pull this one off. Today I want to also tell them that He has so lovingly given me incredible testimonies in my own life over these past eighteen months, in order for me to meditate on and keep focused on, to believe that God will certainly bring me through this time as He's done before.

"God is not a man, that He should lie, Nor a son of man, that He should repent; Has He said, and will He not do it? Or has He spoken, and will He not make it good?" (Numbers 23:19).

"Behold, I am the LORD, the God of all flesh; is anything too difficult for Me?" (Jeremiah 32:27).

"Ah Lord GOD! Behold, You have made the heavens and the earth by Your great power and by Your outstretched arm! Nothing is too difficult for You, who shows lovingkindness to thousands, but repays the iniquity of fathers into the bosom of their children after them, O great and mighty God The LORD of hosts is His name; great in counsel and mighty in deed, whose eyes are open to all the ways of the sons of men, giving to everyone according to his ways and according to the fruit of his deeds" (Jeremiah 32:17–19).

What He reminded me of while meditating and reflecting on the above promises, is that the eagle that flies alone and is so rare, that it gets our attention—eagles, like powerful Christians, are on the endangered species list. That's why it's been my desire to breed more eagles for the Lord: beginning with my own children, as well as each of the women I am blessed to encourage through my ministry and also RMI. Ha, my ministry. This is just one more area that the Lord is having me trust Him for as I watch it dying a slow, quiet and painful death.

Yet, "Truly, truly, I say to you, unless a grain of wheat falls into the earth and dies, it remains alone; but if it dies, it bears much fruit" (John 12:24). It could be that my ministry and my life as I know it now, has to die for it to bear the fruit God intended. This means I will need to believe God through the death until it's time for my life and ministry to be resurrected again.

Precious one, are you determined to believe God for great things right now? If you are, then you must expect to be faced with great and seemingly destructive opposition. Your reputation, the world as you know it, they will all have to be put on the altar day-by-day and moment-by-moment. Your reason for trusting God may change, as mine has, or maybe you are way ahead of me and have had the right reason from the start. For me, I reach this level of belief first, because it was like my very life was on fire like a burning building. I knew that I needed to follow the Lord radically in order to save my children and the women in my ministry.

Once I was safely out of that fire (the divorce), I began radically living for *love.* I was His new bride, and love was my motivator—the "in love" variety. By the time I was traveling internationally, which meant leaving my children for weeks at a time (remember, too, that their father was also gone and I was leaving them alone), I knew that radical, obedient living was what it was going to take to push my family through to what was waiting on the other side for their future. Not only what my zealous life would do for them, but what influence that they might derive from witnessing it.

Just this morning though, I have come to understand my motivation to be a bit different. Today, I see what it's going to take to reach that pinnacle that the Lord is urging me to climb through—His love for me. If I want to believe God for great things, this, my dear, is what it is going to take, and what drives me upward, which has always, and will always be, His love for me and my devotion to Him; this is what matters—it is all that matters.

"I'm asking God for one thing, only one thing: To live with Him in His house my whole life long. [Where] I'll contemplate His beauty; I'll study at His feet" (Psalm 27:4, MSG).

"There's no one quite like you among the gods, O Lord, and nothing to compare with your works. All the nations You made are on their way, ready to give honor to You, O Lord, Ready to put Your beauty on display, parading Your greatness, and the great things You do— You're the One, there's no one but You!" (Psalm 86:8, MSG). Let me be the first to give You the honor and love you deserve in return for all you've done for me, no matter what I lose.

Chapter 8

You're Being Set-Up

The One forming light and creating darkness,
Causing well-being and **creating calamity**;
I am the LORD who does all these.
—Isaiah 45:7

Several times, I have had the urge to write this chapter due to the fact that it seems that each day I see more clearly that I am being set up. Knowing that I am writing to an audience of different cultures around the world, I am not sure all of you clearly understand this term "being set-up." So before I explain how and why we are being set-up (and by whom), I need to establish this concept. A simple definition of being *set-up* is "to cause someone to be caught and blamed for something."

Now that this concept is basically established, I can move on to why I see that this is clearly happening to me, and so that you know it is also (more than likely) happening to you too. Let me begin by saying that for most of us to realize something is happening to us (like being set-up), it very often needs to have happened before. So let me take you back and use just one example that I think easily explains what I mean and how I was able to realize we each are being set-up.

In May of this year, I was just finishing a tour in Asia. I was in Hong Kong for the fifth time and was actually there to enjoy the city before heading back home (after a speaking engagement with the group of women living there who are part of RMI). That morning, I was delighted because I was about to get on my computer to see and speak to my children at a time we'd agreed to meet. After just a few minutes of saying hello, my son stopped me and said, "Dad says he wants to speak to you."

Well, all of you know the feeling—we know we are about to face something new and probably difficult, especially when your ex-husband asks all the children to leave the room. That is when he looked into the computer and calmly told me that he was going to destroy all of the RMI ministry resources (books and videos I'd purchased). Though I had been gone for only a few weeks, my mind visualized the boxes that lined my office and also my garage where we warehoused the rest. [At that time, we were able to save half the price of the books and videos by buying cases at a time, so that's what we'd done; this was prior to my ex leaving.] At that very moment, God was setting me up.

As I have mentioned before in my books, most of us who have been in church for a while have been taught to blame the devil for anything "bad" that happens to us, but the more that I read certain portions of Scriptures (that for some reason never make it onto most pulpits or into most Christian books), and the more I live this abundant life that He died for us to be allowed to live, the more I see that it is God Himself who is setting you and me up.

"That men may know from the rising to the setting of the sun that there is no one besides Me. I am the LORD, and there is no other, The One forming light and creating darkness, causing well-being and *creating calamity*; I am the LORD who does all these" (Isaiah 45:6–7). When you read this, there's really no other way to interpret what it says.

Sometimes it is the enemy who is at work or is asking to sift us as wheat (as he did with the apostle Peter), yet even then— it is God who is just using this demonic figure attempting to do his dirty work—knowing full well it will only prove to be for the *good* of his victim. Remember, the enemy has no power whatsoever, or force equal to that of the believer. "You are from God, little children, and have overcome them; because *greater is He who is in you* than he who is in the **world**" (1 John 4:4). So I have chosen to ignore this infamous little figure just as I do a fly that has gotten into my home—he can be annoying but poses little threat to me. This is how I explained the enemy to my three youngest children as I drove them to church just last week: the enemy is annoying but hardly a threat, just like a pesky fly.

So, with this principle, we can also put the people in our lives (husbands, ex-husbands, our boss, our mean in-laws, or even the attorney who represents them) in this category of those who cannot harm us. "Why are the nations in an uproar and the peoples devising a vain thing? The kings of the earth take their stand and the rulers take counsel together against the LORD and *against His Anointed* . . . He who sits in the heavens *laughs*, the Lord scoffs at them" (Psalms 2:1–4). If he laughs at their futile attempts, no matter how things look, we have the confidence that once the evil has done what it was intended to do, the tides will turn.

Being set-up, as you know by now, first appears as something bad, when in fact, it will *result* in the opposite conclusion—we are actually being set-up by God—in order to be blessed! Now, if we really believed that every adversity was the condition for blessings, not for destruction, and we believe that it was God, not the devil, who was in control, then wouldn't we be able to go *through* it with enthusiasm rather than dread or fear? This is what God continually tries to assure us throughout the Bible, but instead we choose to fear and dread often due to a lack of this principle being taught properly and much more often.

Over these past two years, like never before, I see the incredible happening, as a result of the: tragedy, incredible attacks, and unfair treatment we've faced. False accusations against my character resulted in being set-up, then honored by men and women around the world (and most importantly, for me, honored and respected by my own children). And the destruction of my books also resulted in being set-up. After discussing, and trusting God with Erin, it's what led her to be asked to sign with one of the largest publishers in the world, and the books will be sold and printed on demand (with new videos that are being planned to be played online rather than needing anyone to buy a DVD). Therefore, I (and RMI) will no longer need to purchase in bulk or warehouse or even mail to anyone! The Lord lifted the burden so His brides can spend more time just loving Him and being loved by Him!!

Which is where this newest journey all began, remember? It all began by my losing my restored marriage, once again, cheated on, and also sued by my ex-husband for all I had, which as you know, was simply God setting me up, in order to bless me—finally and completely becoming the Lord's beloved bride—with a honeymoon that took me around the world with Him!!

Of course, the blessed results are also due to having the right response. "But I say to you, do not resist an evil person; but whoever slaps you on your right cheek, turn the other to him also. If anyone wants to sue you and take your shirt, let him have your coat also. Whoever forces you to go one mile, go with him two" (Matthew 5:38–40).

As we discussed in many previous chapters, if we resist an evil or an evil person, we miss what that adversity was sent to do *for* us in the first place. This, as I want to remind you again, is where most Christians live—resisting evil (never mind taking it to the point of receiving the blessing by blessing their attacker). Though many may not even resist outwardly, they're certainly resisting evil in their prayers, which is often where the Christians are focusing their prayers, praying against the evil. So since God does hear our prayers, so often the wave of attacks may subside, but often return again and again, hoping to accomplish why the adversity (and its messenger) was sent. "So shall My Word be which goes forth from My mouth; *it shall not return to Me void,* without **accomplishing** what I desire and without **succeeding** in the matter for which I sent it" (Isaiah 55:11).

Jesus went through the middle of the worst adversity in history and was not delivered from it. Though He prayed that this cup (of adversity) pass from His lips, His desire ultimately was for God's will to be done. This entire principle, that Jesus' life was based on, is one that is entirely overlooked by today's Christian—God's will and not resisting evil. There's no doubt that it is His will that we are each set-up— in order for us to be blessed and as how God will also be glorified.

Examples

It was not until the Israelites were set-up with much more unfair treatment, which by the end of the plagues, concluded their captivity when their captors sent them away with all "articles of silver and articles of gold, and clothing" from their nation leaving it broken and "plundered" (Exodus 12:35–36).

It wasn't **until Joseph was set-up** by his brothers that he was taken captive by Egyptians and he got to Potiphar's house, where he again was set-up by his master's immoral, then rejected wife, that then led him to years of prison. Remember too that Joseph was also set-up by the cupbearer who "did not remember **Joseph,** but forgot him" to spend one more year in prison until God had the Egyptian nation set-up for its famine. All of this set-up was in place to save Joseph's own family and to make Joseph ruler of the nation just under Pharaoh.

There are many women of the Bible who were also set-up for greatness.

Ruth was set-up through the death of her husband, father-in-law, *and* brother-in-law so that there were no men in her life just so that she would be favored in that particular field where she gathered a few kernels in order for her and her mother-in-law to survive. And where her future began, meeting her husband, Boaz, and was part of the lineage of Jesus Himself.

Esther was set-up to be the new wife of the king in order for the Jewish people to be saved (and so that her faithful cousin, Mordecai, could be honored as well).

Even **Mary, the mother of Jesus, was set-up** as a young, unmarried, pregnant girl to be "blessed among women" as the virgin mother of our Savior.

God didn't put all those examples in the Bible for us not to get Who set these great men and women of faith up—and for what purpose! The purpose of evil (in the life of the believer) and why God sets us up is, again, for us to be blessed and for Him to get the glory He deserves.

So, dear one, all the adversity and all that evil that is coming against you today, rejoice! This is a set-up—God is about to bless you!!

"Beloved, **do not be surprised at the fiery ordeal** among you, which comes upon you for your testing, as though some strange thing were happening to you; but to the degree that you share the sufferings of Christ, keep on rejoicing; so that also at the revelation of His glory, you may rejoice with exultation" (1 Peter 4:12).

"I have told you these things, so that in me you may have peace. In this world **you *will* have trouble.** But take heart! I have *overcome* the world" (John 16:33). Thank You Lord!!

———— Chapter 9 ————

What's the Point?

But if any of you lacks wisdom
let him ask of God who gives it to men liberally.
—James 1:5

What did I do it all for? What was the point? Did I really **lose** as most people think, or was I really the winner?

Normally when I begin writing a chapter, I begin with the title. It's almost as if He's giving me direction for where He wants me to go as I begin writing. Though I believe I know what I want to share with you, where I'm headed, I am still not clear how to sum it up enough to create a suitable title. Nevertheless, I will set off and simply trust that the Lord will help me share this wonderful revelation with you, title or not.

If you've read any of Erin's books, you certainly must have stumbled onto *A Wise Woman,* which originally was created for the desperate women who, like myself, had found themselves abandoned or cheated on by their husbands. It was a culmination of what the Lord had revealed to Erin during her two-year restoration journey when she sought God to restore her marriage. From that book, she explains that a smaller book was pulled out to help those women to simply get out of their crisis (once again who had been abandoned or whose husbands had been unfaithful to them), again like me, that was entitled *How God Can and Will Restore Your Marriage.*

After using both books, as most of you know, my marriage was restored, and even before it was, I'd begun helping Erin with her books and online ministry. But, when my husband left me a second time, suddenly, after fourteen years of restoration, many women thought that I had **lost** big time, and I also felt disqualified to help

Erin so I resigned! Some women I'd been working with even went so far as to accuse me of being a fake before I resigned, saying that *if* I had been the wife that I professed to trying to be, following *A Wise Woman,* and encouraging other women to also follow the principles, basically saying that if I was "practicing what I preached," my husband would not have left me.

Thankfully, through false accusations and out of his own mouth, my ex-husband actually defended me to our senior pastor as "the perfect wife" and later confessed that he also had (prior to how I handled his leaving a second time) thought I was a fake, but that I was "unbelievably real." Wow, only God, my dear, only God could have prompted him to say that. And of course, Erin said she knew the real me, and one or two other very close friends affirmed their belief in me. But due to what happened, I began to doubt my calling as a minister or of having anything more to say to any woman.

Once the dust settled, and the initial crisis of the second divorce, additional lawsuits he filed, and the initial financial ruin had died down (of course I never defended myself), then I, too, had questions like "What was it all for? Why did I learn to be that "perfect" wife *if* I was to have no husband after all? What would I do now since my testimony was gone, who could I ever minister to that would listen?"

Revelations

Fast forward. It's now been about a year and a half since the divorce was final, so I have been living without a "husband" for many months now. During my many days and hours of traveling around the world, the Lord has since revealed to me many answers that I believe many of you are struggling with as well. Those of you, who like me, began this course of action to restore your marriage, but you, like me, are without a restoration or a husband in the home and are wondering: What was the point? Even worse, you are feeling as if you are a failure. Because come on, aren't those women who write their "restored testimonies" the winners? Doesn't that then make you, and now me, the losers?

Today, let me dispel this myth and reveal to you the truth that will set you free—free to rejoice and be glad!

We not only did *not* lose, darling, we won!

The very purpose of this transformation He made in us wasn't to be anyone's wife, but in order for us to be His forever bride—a bride of a Prince—the Prince of Peace! Doesn't that mean, then, that you and I are a princess? Yes! And this means that for eternity you are promised (by Someone who is unable to lie) to be treated and cherished like a bride who is loved beyond imagination. "God can do anything, you know—far more than you could ever imagine or guess or request in your wildest dreams!" (Ephesians 3:20 The Message).

Each day and in every new season of my life, I am learning this truth in amazing ways!! May I share with you the most recent?

The Lord told me in late March of this year that in six months, which would be September, that my life would be totally different. To confirm this, He told me "something totally unbelievable would happen the following month," April. Sure enough, instead of us, RMI, publishing their own books, they were picked up by a huge publisher, a secular one, who will be printing and distributing them. This is incredible due to the destroyed books I mentioned in the previous chapter, so that wherever I was, anywhere traveling around the world, I could simply mail anyone a copy of any of the books that changed my life! Also by trying to stop part of my ongoing income (of selling RMI books), which I believe he'd destroyed to cripple me financially in order to take custody of my younger children—God had a bigger plan for allowing this.

If you've followed the history of RMI, Erin has explained that years ago when their first publisher could not keep up with the demand, they tried *unsuccessfully* to get any Christian publisher to print even one of their books! Over and over again they were rejected due to Christian book publishers believing they were too radical—and as we know, the only books that speak and share the truth! So that's why RMI began to self-publish their books. So to have a secular company "publish ten titles to start with" is truly remarkable.

"Now glory be to God, who by his mighty power at work within us is able to do far more than we would ever dare to ask or even dream of—infinitely beyond our highest prayers, desires, thoughts, or hopes" (Ephesians 3:20 TLB).

"Therefore the LORD longs to be gracious to you, and therefore He WAITS on high to have compassion on you. For the LORD is a God of *justice;* how blessed are all those who long for Him" (Isaiah 30:18).

This new turn of events, that affected me as much as it affected Erin and RMI, made me wait with great expectation for what September would hold. Funny thing is (and we all do it) I imagined *exactly* how I was going to be blessed. I was sure it had to be in the area of my finances since surely He had to show up there! So that's what I was waiting and anticipating until October 1st arrived. For the next week, I tried to make sense of it all. I often thought of writing a chapter about how Lazarus and his sisters must have had difficulty waiting for Jesus to arrive until it *seemed* it was too late (but how God had set them all up for a greater miracle by letting him die—but that's another chapter). Since, instead of my finances increasing, my finances are in fact still dying a slow death. Nevertheless, I have been reminded by the Lord (often enough) to ponder the story of Lazarus when I speak to Him about how bleak my finances look. So it may be the Lazarus chapter is coming. However, this is not what this chapter is about, nor for how my life was going to change.

Without ever realizing it, my life did change, dramatically! But would you believe I almost missed it? It was ever so subtle that the enormity of it all eluded me. You know, I think that is what happened to so many of the Jews who were waiting for Jesus, their Messiah, to arrive. He came in with such subtlety, in a manger and a carpenter's son, so since they imagined Him to coming as a royal earthly king (with all the splendor), many of the Jews missed it, missed Him entirely.

What was it? Subtly, suddenly and incredibly, I realized I'd simply become a stay-at-home mom! I woke up one morning to the fact that He'd given me the desires of my heart that I had wanted since before I had my first child. Throughout my marriage, I had either worked part-time or had helped my husband with him in his profession and even when he'd become a pastor. So you ask (as I did)—how is this possible when I am a single mom of so many children, with no child support, and certainly not independently wealthy?

"Behold, I am the LORD, the God of all flesh; is anything too difficult for Me?" (Jeremiah 32:27). "Ah Lord GOD! Behold, You have made the heavens and the earth by Your great power and by Your outstretched arm! Nothing is too difficult for You!" (Jeremiah 32:17).

At first, I could not accept this blessing as real. Certainly I would have to "work"— right? Come on, again, let's be real here. Yet, over and over again the Lord reminded me of my over 25 years of marriage, how He had trained me to be that "perfect wife," and this was the reason. I was now not just His wife, but His bride. So would He expect or want *His* bride to "work"? BUT, what about my failing finances? The Lord asked me one day, "Michele, if you learned not to question your earthly husband about the condition of the family finances, and you trusted him with the solution and the burden, why then are you concerned now when you have a heavenly Husband who has unlimited resources?" Wow, this certainly helped me to see things differently!

The Lord has graciously worked it out, also, I am doing all the things I love to do! Rather than a job to make money, I am free to write, and to continue to minister to women! Even the lack of finances plays a part in it too. If I were drawing a salary, then I would feel too guilty to do what I am doing; however, the little bit that is coming in is just enough to keep my life going. And ministering to me is never work— it's my passion. And though I believed that my no longer having a restored marriage disqualified me from having a ministry, the truth turned out to be that having a restored marriage only limited my ministering. Every woman alive needs His love and deserves to be His bride! Not everyone needs or wants a restored marriage—so by losing my life (as I knew it) I found my life!!

"Then Jesus said to His disciples, 'If anyone wishes to come after Me, let him deny himself, and take up his cross, and follow Me. For whoever wishes to save his life shall lose it; but whoever loses his life for My sake shall find it'" (Matthew 16:25).

So what about you? What was His purpose in your not being a wife right now; besides letting you experience Him as the Husband of your dreams? I believe it is ultimately to give you the desires of your heart—desires that you may have even forgotten over the years! It's so easy to lose our focus when the journey of our life takes us on a path we thought we would never take. Nevertheless, God did hear and remember each and every one of those desires and hasn't forgotten one, not one.

So precious one, ask the Lord to show you what He has been up to and what you may have missed. I believe that many of you are actually living the life that your dreams have always been made of.

Chapter 10

From the Inside Out

Moreover, I will give you a **new heart**
and put a **new** spirit within you . . .
—Ezekiel 36:26

It was just last week that I was marveling at how the Lord had healed me from a most horrendous "wound of the heart" that had been festering for years. Most of you are also nursing deep sores or dealing with painful scarring from your past: some from your childhood, others from your difficult marriage. Some of you, I know, are seeking help from psychology methods that may seem to work, but in the end will result in being healed superficially.

"They heal the brokenness of the daughter of My people **superficially**, saying, 'Peace, peace,' but there is no peace" (Jeremiah 8:11).

Though I never tried any sort of psychology or their methods, I did try in vain to get help from someone other than the Lord, so my pain and sores oozed for many, many years—it was tragic—tragic because I could have gone to the Lord when they were fresh and been completely healed. Even now I wonder why I waited to take it to the Great Physician. Dear one, have you been suffering with something because you have neglected to take it to the One who can heal you from the inside out?

Personally, my pain stemmed from not being accepted by my husband's family since the day that we married; I actually had never even met them when we eloped. When he telephoned after the ceremony, my excitement grew to dread as I could hear him consoling his mom; then he put me on the phone and all she did was cry. His father and brother also "welcomed" me to the family about the same way minus the tears.

The first time I met his family it was almost a year later when I was already pregnant with our first son. Though they tried to be nice . . . well, we all can sense when we are not accepted or wanted. It didn't take long to hear that they had wanted my husband to marry someone else, but more importantly to them, they wanted him to finish college first before settling down. There were many other issues they had, all of them were valid; nevertheless, the rejection and lack of acceptance played a major role in our marriage troubles and woes.

To add to the dilemma, we lived hours away by plane, which only helped to keep the obvious rejection to telephone calls and infrequent visits, but it also served as a way to keep me from gaining that place of acceptance since we did live so far away from each other.

In my ignorance and stupidity (for over twenty years) I had tried in vain to get help from my husband to close the gap with his family. Since I had helped him gain a great relationship with my family (who initially didn't accept him), I figured that he should do the same for me. Yet I never realized the principle until I took it to Him, when He showed me, "They for their part may turn to you, but as for you, you must not turn to them . . ." to which the Lord then led me to add "for help or healing" (Jeremiah 15:19). Even with this verse, I did not get it at first.

By going to my husband for comfort rather than the Lord all those years, instead of help, or sympathy, or support, I got (time after time after time) insults added to the injury. He blamed the problem on me and justified his family's opinion of me. I truly believed what my husband said about me until I took it to the Lord and asked if it was true. The Lord immediately opened my eyes and asked me if I was able to get along with people. As I pondered this, the Lord then asked me who I had failed to get along with (other than my in-laws) and I was not able to think of even one other person who I was unable to win over. It was then that He told me that this issue was on their end, not mine, but it still hurt. I know that you know what I mean.

Looking back, today I am totally baffled that I failed to understand that no one could help me gain their acceptance or to get a better relationship with them. And there was no one who could heal my past hurts: not me, not therapy, not even gaining their approval would heal the deep wounds. It was the moment I'd hurt enough that I finally ran to God, my Father, in my suffering. Are you there yet my love? Even if you can bear a bit more, why suffer when you can begin to heal right now?

To begin the healing process God opened my eyes to such incredible wisdom about my situation. "But if any of you *lacks wisdom,* let him ask of God, who gives to all generously and without reproach, and it will be given to him" (James 1:5). First, God reminded me that my husband and I were very different people with different personalities. I had expected him to build me up in his family's eyes as I had done for him with my family. Seems logical, but once I asked, once I came to Him for help, He showed me that in my family I am the peacemaker and am sought after to smooth things over; my husband was not like that (very few men are). So all those years of assuming he could or should help was foolish.

Next, God revealed to me that it wasn't only me that my in-laws disliked and didn't accept—sadly, I woke up to the truth—they did not like or accept their own son (my husband at the time). So if they didn't like or accept him, why would they like or accept me? Finally, God let me feel my husband's pain of not having that acceptance with his own parents. He reminded me that I had been so incredibly loved by my parents and was beyond accepted—my family openly cherished me. So why did I expect more when my husband didn't have this basic need fulfilled?

Yet we all do, don't we? We want it all. And that sort of selfishness and self-centeredness, for years, could have led to a slippery slope. Often while in my misery, it would trigger the thoughts of all those other guys that I had turned down when they asked me to marry them and how *their* family thought I was so wonderful. My goodness—so foolish! This kind of looking back to the "what ifs" just added to the pain and suffering, and as I said could have led me to acting on those feelings. It's only by the grace of God I didn't. These, my precious, are those thoughts that should be immediately cast down as you run to Him. However, it is clear that the Lord used this ongoing misery, along with every other suffering in my life, as His way of refining me and letting me know Him more intimately, to share with you today.

Yes, all things did work out for good. Today I am free of pain and suffering with an awesome testimony! Let me continue . . .

With the wisdom and God's viewpoint replacing my own, my healing was well on its way. But before I tell you what God told me to do, you must promise to not try this "method" in your own situation (even if it's very similar to mine) because what the Lord wants you to do is to come to Him to get your own prescription, not use mine. This is why God allows us to go through things, so that we can begin to hear Him and fellowship with Him. Agreed?

What the Lord told me to do seemed so simple, too simple—He simply told me to write a short note to my mother-in-law and one to my father-in-law each week.

The first time I sat down to write I stopped and cringed, remembering how I had "tried" that to help them get to know me; only to be scolded by my husband when his mom called him complaining that I'd written to brag about *my* children. I was stunned, since I'd basically written the same letter to my own parents who were thrilled. So when I stopped to ask Him, He reminded me that my parents adored me, and in turn, they adored my children. Telling them every wonderful thing that they each did, therefore, was a delight.

So, dear one, here is another point in your healing: be sure to tell the Lord any apprehensions that you have; He is always ready with more wisdom and understanding when our hearts are open. When fear is standing in our way, again, don't tell others your concerns—take them each to the Lord so He can rid you of your fears, helping you to do what you sensed He's asked.

For me, the Lord remedied this uneasiness of not "bragging," by showing me a vision of the tiny note cards I had in my drawer. He said that by using something very small, that it would easily not allow for much writing at all. All He said I was to do is to "keep in touch." So I wrote my first two notes, put them in the mail and felt better. And so I wouldn't have to think about it, He led me to set up a notification on my computer so that every Wednesday I would write without fail. Another immediate change in me was that I finally felt no need to speak to my husband about the plan. This was a huge change. I realized, after going to Him again and again, that this was between the Lord and me. What a turning point, not to feel I needed to mention when I discovered something that I knew would change my life. I'd finally realized that to share the Lord's plan with anyone else would often result in others mocking the simple idea or tell me what I should do instead.

So for almost two years, each week, I wrote my little note cards. The results began just a few weeks later when my mother-in-law began writing in return; however, she would not send them directly to me, but would address them to our family. This, at first, made my husband wonder why she was writing instead of calling like she'd always done, but again I had finally learned, too, about the blessings of that quiet spirit in so many situations where I'd always said far too much instead of just remaining quiet.

My father-in-law, on the other hand, never acknowledged my letters at all, which surprisingly was really fine with me. It didn't matter what anyone else did at this point, what I knew was that this was God's prescription for my healing—nothing more, nothing less. It wasn't until my husband was visiting his dad that he saw my letter at the top of a stack of his mail and was a bit shocked when he handed him the letter from me, and his dad said, "Oh, she writes every week," and put it down without opening or reading it. Once my husband got home he questioned me about it, to which I gave a very short response since the Lord told me to prepare an answer. When he asked why I hadn't told him, I simply said, "Oh, because it was between them and me to gain a better relationship." Not only was I healing, but also the Lord was giving me more of that "quiet spirit" that I longed to have since it was so precious in the sight of God, along with wisdom I'd learned but didn't really know how to apply like from 1 Peter 3:13-15, "Who is there to harm you if you prove zealous for what is good? But even if you should suffer for the sake of righteousness, you are blessed and do not fear their intimidation, and do not be troubled, but sanctify Christ as Lord in your hearts, *always being **ready*** to make a defense to everyone who **asks** you to give an account for the hope that is in you, yet with *gentleness* and ***reverence.***"

How many of you, precious ones, continually, as I did for so many years, share your heart and your pain with others only to add more pain and suffering, then often adding insults to your injuries? Once again, what He longs to do is be gracious to you, to help you, to heal you and to comfort you. Then, when we have spent time with Him, laying it all out, even concerns we have for following His prescription, our healing will begin. Then, just as important, we must hide, treasure and ponder these things in our hearts, rather than sharing them with others—giving us time to heal. "But Mary treasured all these things, pondering them in her heart" (Luke 2:19).

If we fail to keep these treasures hidden until our healing is complete, it can be compared to having a broken bone set, then having it re-broken by cruel words or mocking. Or having a gaping wound sewn up, only to have those delicately placed stitches torn apart.

Instead, learn from Mary, treasure and hide what the Lord tells you, hold it deep in your heart and ponder the truths often. And, once again, it will be the gentle and quiet spirit that wins out above all else, "But let it be the hidden person of the heart, with the imperishable quality of a *gentle and **quiet** spirit*, which is precious in the sight of God" (1 Peter 3:4).

One day my prescription of weekly note writing ended, it was the day after my husband walked in to our bedroom to announce he was headed to the attorney to divorce me. As it had done for almost three years, my computer notification came up to write to my in-laws. So I stopped to ask the Lord if I was to continue writing to them, to which He answered, "It is finished." To my utter amazement, I realized at that moment that there was absolutely no more pain, no more sorrow. There was no open sore, nor was there even the tiniest scar from years and years of pain beyond hope!

Having everything "work out for good" falls so short of my gratitude to the Lord. Hundreds of times since my divorce, I have thought about how easy it has been to not be emotionally tied to my in-laws since, now that I am no longer married to their son. Many of you, however, are close to your in-laws, and to lose them has become doubly hard. For you, dear one, come away from this chapter feeling how easy it would be if you were like me and not attached to the in-laws. Don't rehearse or share with others how you miss them—falling into self-pity for your loss, which is very dangerous. Instead, realize that your cure, like mine, comes directly from seeking God, and also your Mighty and compassionate Physician, who has your perfect prescription written and waiting for you—if you would simply sit at His feet and ask. "Therefore the LORD longs to be gracious to you, and therefore He waits on high to have compassion on you. For the LORD is a God of justice; how blessed are all those who long for Him" (Isaiah 30:18).

Now for the epilog: The title for this chapter was already on my notes when I had the most amazing thing happen. It has been more than sixteen months since my divorce was final when I got a letter from my ex-mother-in-law *begging* me to forgive her. She said that I would always be her daughter-in-law, and that she wanted us to begin writing to each other again. Have you ever noticed that it is not until we no longer are desperate for something (apart from desperate for the Lord and His love) that we finally get what we thought we could not live without?

Not knowing what to do about this letter, I went into my bedroom to talk to the Lord about what He wanted me to do. Ladies, that's when I realized I was set-up (see chapter 8). Rather than writing back to her, the Lord told me to send my ex-husband an email asking him to handle this with his mom. Since forgiveness also means that we forget, I was shocked when my ex-husband wrote back with the same venomously cruel words I had experienced for years! Baffled, once again I retreated to my bedroom to seek the Lord for wisdom (and comfort this time) to know where I'd gone wrong. Lovingly, the Lord told me that, yes, indeed I was set up so that the pain of rejection was fresh so that I could easily write this chapter with much more feeling—but that is not all. Now that I understand and live the principle of overcoming evil with good, going the extra mile, and really blessing my enemies—I was also being set up for a blessing—by blessing my ex-husband *and* my ex-mother-in-law!

First, He led me to reply to my ex-husband's email with how right he was, and to thank him for his help! In his email my ex-husband was quick to also criticize my ministry, and especially me as a minister, saying "that I was missing an opportunity to have a 'restored relationship' testimony to share (referring to my ex-mother-in-law." In addition, I'd sensed he'd been watching me, so I'd asked the Lord if I was paranoid or imaging then. So, by following His lead (of asking him to handle the situation with his mom), God revealed that he had been visiting my marriage website, and also often coming to RMI to read praise reports (since he made references to both of them). This also made me realize that He was showing me creative ways of becoming more discreet.

Precious one, I know I am not the only one who is being mocked and questioned about what you are doing. If you are not hiding things in your heart, if you are not going to Him for your already written prescription, if you are hoping your method or someone else's will heal you or relieve any pain, I'm hoping that what I've shared with you will change the way you think and act on healing your hurts. Many of you are questioning yourself right now due to what others have said to you or about you. Beloved, before taking any cruel words to heart, take these statements to the Lord to see what He says about them, just as I did (that I'm going to speak more about in the next chapter.) But for now, let me share the conclusion of this epilog...

As I was replying to my mother-in-law, the Lord reminded me of something I'd read earlier that morning. I was ministering to a woman who, like myself, had a husband who had remarried. On the website, it said, "though we do emphasize restoring relationships, we do not encourage an ex-wife to foster a relationship with former in-laws, when her ex-husband has remarried. We, at all times, must always think of others as more important than ourselves." "Do not be overcome with evil but overcome evil with good" (Romans 12:21). That's when I knew what He was asking me, and letting me do.

Rather than continuing to write her, as she asked, instead I replied to my mother-in-law, and I included a check for her to take her *new* daughter-in-law out to lunch so she knows that she, alone, is her daughter-in-law now.

When I began writing this chapter (which I started but it sat for a while), I was expecting her letters to stop. However, it continued twice more. My ex-mother-in-law began to send me money, and the second time I replied, I doubled the amount, then asked her to instead take my ex-husband's new wife out to lunch based on, "But I say to you, do not resist him who is evil; but whoever slaps you on your right cheek, turn to him the other also. And if anyone wants to sue you, and take your shirt, let him have your coat also. And whoever shall force you to go one mile, go with him two" (Matthew 5:39-41).

Isn't it always exciting to see God at work in our lives and in the lives of others? It is not enough to simply turn the other cheek; the real blessing comes from blessing those who have for years despitefully used or persecuted you, and then continue when you thought the relationship was over. It often goes beyond reasoning—you are able, through the experience, to actually feel the Lord's love pulsating inside your heart. And that's when you realize that every pain and/or ill feeling is totally gone, having been replaced by a power so magnificent that it saved us while we were yet sinners—this power is His love.

The final letter was sent, when once again, she wrote sending me money. And as before, I took it to the Lord to know what He wanted me to do. In my final letter I doubled the double, asking my ex-mother-in-law to take her new daughter-in-law and also her four new grandchildren (my ex-husband's step children) out for pizza. He had me end my letter by letting her know that I didn't feel right about our writing, knowing how it could potentially hurt her new daughter-in-law and the new marriage, and then thanking her for being such a wonderful ex-mother-in-law to me. So I would lovingly think of that by no longer opening or reading any further letters from her. Thankfully, I have not heard from her since that time.

What has or may transpire is not something I choose to think about because I know God is working behind the scenes, and whatever is going on doesn't concern me. My only concern is and should be, how I remain focused on my new and beautiful Husband who also just happens to be the most awesome Physician, drenched in His love, as He continues to love me and heal me from the inside out.

———— Chapter 11 ————

Guilty of All

For whoever keeps the whole law
and yet stumbles in one point,
he has become **guilty of all**.
—James 2:10

What makes any of us think that we can measure up?

When will our works finally die its final death, allowing us the freedom of living Abundantly all due to His grace and based solely on His love?

One of the slowest deaths I've watched, sometimes in horror, has been how my finances have been under attack. Throughout this book I have openly shared about the rollercoaster my finances have taken, each helping me to understand and trust Him with wherever this is going. Today, more than ever, I am confident that God is about to do something and He adamantly will share His glory with no one when He does it. That's why He allows our *works* of the flesh to come to ruin. Even the subtlest effort on my part or yours will never succeed, praise God.

The most recent turn of events happened on Saturday. I was blessed to entertain a friend of mine, my neighbor, in my home. This is really quite new to me since I may have shared that while married, my ex-husband was not at all comfortable with me having my having friends visit or even having personal friends at all, believing instead, that he should be the only friend I needed. My new Husband, not surprisingly, believes differently! Are we not blessed to have a Husband like this?!?!

While she was visiting we had a wonderful time fellowshipping, discussing the Lord mostly. What struck me as funny, "He who sits in the heavens laughs" (Psalm 2:4) was it just so happened that she came by while my ex-husband was here visiting our children. We actually became friends when I was looking to refinance my house after my divorce; something my husband told me I needed to do. And since, at the time, we were not yet legally divorced, I'd submitted to refinancing my home. Just before she left, we began talking about financial wisdom, things I should and should not do regarding building a firm foundation for a solid financial future.

So while helping me, all of a sudden she mentioned something that she said "never to do" that I had actually begun doing while traveling. Again I had to laugh, which I did out loud, when I told her that I had violated one of the most basic financial principles. My friend sat there shocked, not only because of what I said I did, but because I was laughing about it! My first cause for amusement was because I immediately realized that the Lord was setting me up. Yes, at first, it may have looked like I was being set up for destruction, but in reality, once anything looks hopeless, I knew His setting me up was actually to set me up for a blessing, a real financial miracle!

Guess what? Due to my *tiny* technicality, because of this little mistake I'd made, my dear friend and neighbor explained she would not be able to help me refinance my house. Basically, I found out when attempting to refinance my home, the reason I was denied was that my ex had ruined my financial reputation as part of the divorce. It seems he'd filed additional papers (that I was unaware of), by filing a substantial "judgment" against me. Ultimately, she said it would ruin my financial portfolio for a full ten years.

Since it was my ex who wanted me to get the house refinanced, I explained to him that the papers showed that he had time to withdraw his judgment, explaining the long term affects this would have on me (and the children). Though he immediately agreed, a day or two later he called back to say his attorney had warned him against trusting me. So the judgment will undoubtedly go through, therefore I will await the opportunity for how He wants me to bless him. Though it's natural to want to resist or do something, living supernaturally is what

He told us to do, "But I say to you, do not resist an evil person; but whoever slaps you on your right cheek, turn the other to him also. If anyone wants to sue you and take your shirt, let him have your coat also. Whoever forces you to go one mile, go with him two. Give to him who asks of you, and do not turn away from him who wants to borrow from you" (Matthew 5:39-42). "To sum up, all of you be harmonious, sympathetic, brotherly, kindhearted, and humble in spirit; not returning evil for evil or insult for insult, but giving a blessing instead; for you were called for the very purpose that you *might* **inherit a blessing"** (1 Peter 3:8-9).

Knowing I had to wait for Him to reveal how to bless my ex, I turned my focus on the news of my tiny technicality, when the Lord revealed an exciting truth I'd like to share. The Lord revealed to me that you and I should never, ever, *try* to do anything to help Him, because if we do, it robs Him of the glory that needs to accompany our testimony when it arrives in our life. He is determined to prove this principle: "For by *grace* you have been saved through **faith**; and that not of yourselves, it is the ***gift*** of God; not as a result of works, so that no one may boast" (Ephesians 2:8–9). God graciously saves us day-by-day from each and every one of our trials, when anything is coming against us—as His "gift" based on His love for us, not based on how we earned it. It's just like our salvation, our works didn't and don't help. Why? So that we cannot boast that we had anything to do with it! And it also helps when sharing our testimony so anyone and everyone can receive what they need from a loving and giving Father.

What He showed me, based on what I'd ignorantly done was that—I was guilty of all—due to one tiny technicality. It means that I will never be able to get out from under my ever growing, huge financial crises, which should be terrifying me, but in all honesty, it's not. Instead it's proves that, once again, only God will be able to turn this mess around and dig me out of the debt that is about to bury me. Only God will be able to bless me to the point that I will have a testimony to share with others who are also facing financial ruin (maybe even due to a divorce like mine). As crazy as it sounds, it simply just makes me smile.

Funny, too, that it caused me to seek Him for another way to bless my ex-husband (who just happened to be visiting), blessing him by not keeping his word to withdraw the judgment against me. The Lord showed me that a new detail like this could potentially be one of those "little foxes" that Song of Solomon warns us about that "spoil the vine."

So rather than risk it, I happily sought the Lord for how I might bless him right away, since it was he who put me (and our family) in this precarious position.

Without hesitation or postponing, immediately after envisioning what He was leading me to do, I got up and began walking down the hallway, and when I turned the corner, there he was, so I could easily tell him what I sensed the Lord was asking me to do. What I told him was that each time he was here visiting that I wanted him to be the parent, making the decisions and plans with the children, while I would basically retreat to my room. Instead of sulking about my situation and financial ruin, I found that it actually gave me a mini-honeymoon with my Beloved—so I was really doubly blessed!! To say that my ex-husband was more than just baffled is an understatement, as he stammered and stuttered a "thank you" while I went in and closed my door, leaving him standing in the hallway stunned.

In my experience with dealing with our "enemies," it is not enough to simply "take it" gracefully or humbly (not resisting evil). We must follow through, going beyond just not resisting it, and seek God for how we are to *give a blessing* that is comparable in value or worth. It is only then that our pain or bitterness of heart is replaced with living a life in *paradise*—not simply experiencing a burst of joy or peace. And the only way to find the right blessing to give, is to ask the Lord what to give.

Please, precious one, don't fall short of **blessing** your enemies due to fear of what you might lose (even if it is your self-respect). **It is in the giving that you gain, in the humbling that you are exalted**. This is the only part we play in our developing testimony. It is *not* how we follow every principle to the letter, it is a heart matter, how we're willing to surrender everything and realize that only God is able to fully deliver us or heal us.

My hope is that my financial testimony, as it develops, proves that even when we are extremely careful to follow **all** the principles we've learned, we can easily lose or become disqualified by a simple *tiny* technicality, something easily missed or overlooked. And that it means we are simply **guilty of all** because none of us is perfect. Only the Lord is perfect and has the power, plan, and ability to save and deliver us from that valley we find ourselves in. Now that He has revealed this powerful promise to us once again, let us all simply rest in His love while we trust Him with all the details of our lives!

——————— Chapter 12 ———————

Every Encumbrance

Lay aside every encumbrance and the sin
which so easily entangles us.
—Hebrews 12:1

Most of us know or have heard someone refer to this verse: "Therefore, since we have so great a cloud of witnesses surrounding us, let us also lay aside **every *encumbrance*** and the ***sin*** which so easily entangles us, and let us run with endurance the race that is set before us, fixing our eyes on Jesus, the author and perfecter of faith . . ." (Hebrews 12:1–2). Though we have heard it, I'm sure that we all would agree that the *encumbrance* and the *sin* spoken about is our own. However, just recently I found myself in a web of encumbrances that were not my own, which made me look at this principle in a whole new light.

Today as never before, we see women (and some men) openly share their problems and personal sins with the world via television, and more recently, on social media. Often there is an audience full of people, mostly women, who are shouting (or posting) their opinions, many of whom are quickly given a microphone or platform to voice their outrage or simply tell that person what they should do or not do. On television, the host or hostess (or judge) appears to have the final word and has come to be viewed as an expert on solving the social ills being flaunted before countless, obsessive "can't-get-enough" eyes and ears.

Without realizing it, these shows and social media have adversely affected all our lives by encouraging us to flaunt our own sins, and the sins of others, with our family, friends, neighbors, and even perfect strangers. By participating, we soon find ourselves entangled in a multitude of problems and sins, others and our own, which are weighing **us** down and stealing **our** joy. Not only does it begin by stealing our peace, but it also erodes our beliefs and morals, because who we hang around with is ultimately who we will become.

Encumbered and Entangled

Just last week I submitted a testimony about my sister's healing. I explained that the director of her group home had called me about my sister's problem with depression and they wanted me to commit her to a psychiatric hospital, so I immediately sought God for wisdom. He then prompted me to ask Him for "the source" and we soon discovered that the depression was due to the medication she was taking, for depression! However, it was soon after they stopped the medication she'd become dependent on, when she then could not sleep, so she would call me each morning to complain (and in a way blame me for her lack of sleep). Sound familiar?

Whenever we get involved in other people's problems, we soon will become entangled, and then we find ourselves caught in a web of their encumbrances mixed with our own difficulties we already have to deal with. Once I'd helped my sister and became involved, I found that her director and all the other residences were also "helping" her with more advice about different medications, and many wanted her to see a counselor for her depression. Well, you get the picture: one problem became a web of problems, filled with chaos and confusion.

As my sister's caregiver, I don't have the luxury of stepping away and am somewhat involved, however, it's important that I am careful not to get caught. In this chapter, I want to encourage all of us to take a step back to try to see just how many webs we are caught in, which we need to seek God to free us from: with family, friends, neighbors and coworkers. Today you may realize you're still caught in the sins of your ex-husband, his girlfriend, etc. as you find you're thinking about their problems, and then enlarging the web by discussing these with your own friends or family. It could be your older children who are not where they should be in their spiritual or financial life that is entangling you. Maybe it's your aging parents, or possibly what is happening while your younger children are visiting their dad (and her!).

This is what I found in my own life that was robbing me of intimacy with the Lord. Even after He'd trained me to quickly give Him all *my* problems, asking Him to take care of anything that causes me even the *slightest* problem or concern, I'd unknowingly been doing this with the problems that were not mine.

Just so you know how I've been doing this with my own problems, it's simple to learn. When any problem or concern comes to my mind (like when I wake up and don't know what I am going to do that day about something), I just say, "Darling, I am going to need you to take care of (whatever) for me today. Thank you my Love." Then I move on to talk about something else, usually, telling Him how much I love Him and often we talk about all the wonderful things He did for me the day before.

After I get up, when I'm walking by something in my home that is giving me trouble, like a repair that needs fixing or a cleaning dilemma (like the carpet on my stairs), I just mention it to Him, and again, tell Him I am waiting for Him to show me what to do. Then I simply wait and trust Him, and if it comes to mind again, I'll simply give it to Him again and again. Most of us were taught in *A Wise Woman* to tell our earthly husband that we trust him, so do the same with your heavenly Husband because He loves to hear it too.

Nevertheless, even though I've been freed of the millions of my own dilemmas, the temptation kept trying to trip me up with other people's problems, especially my own children's. Since I now have children who are adults (over the age of 18), it is easier for me to encourage them to find their own solution, allowing me not to become entangled. However, like many of you, I still have younger children living at home, so this is where I found myself being pulled in. In seeking God for wisdom, He reminded me that with my older children, I've always tried to use these as opportunities to share scriptural principles that I live in my own life. And I've also tried to be careful to make sure that they are who makes the final decision of what to do (especially, to seek the Lord for the answer), doing it for themselves—rather than me becoming entangled with the decision, which must rest with them. Not just say it does, but make sure it does.

Thankfully, after showing me this, just this weekend the Lord led me to do the very same thing with my youngest daughter who is just ten. She has been getting a lot of pressure from her dad to move and live with him, full time; with him and his wife and her children, and has been saying it's where she wants to live. While on the other side, I am getting just as much pressure from my older children to stop this from happening, as they tell me if I only knew what is "really going on up there" I'd stop her.

This is when I took the opportunity to remind each of them about the principle of the father and the prodigal: how the father actually encouraged the son to have what he said he wanted by giving him his inheritance (ahead of time), and that he actually knew and acknowledged it would be to further his son's sin. (Read Luke 15:11-32.) I explained that the reason God shows us this parable was to show us how not getting in the way of others is the quickest and surest way, for any person, to find that what they *thought* they wanted was not worth what they'll eventually lose. Of course, I also reminded them that God does not get in our way when we want what is wrong, and the verse in Psalm 1 says this clearly, "Blessed is the man who walks not in the counsel of the wicked, nor stands in the way of sinners..." (Psalm 1:1 ESV). These sessions with my older children serve to remind them, and me, of the principles that have been overlooked and untaught by the church.

Then, yesterday, again, I was being nudged into another entanglement by one of my sons who did not want me to lend any more money to his older brother who he believed had become financially irresponsible. I had to tell him, once again, that the Lord had told me to "give freely" whenever *asked* while reminding my son (who'd voiced his concern) that God would turn everything around for good for all parties. Already the Lord revealed that the financial entanglement that he had fallen into had kept him from moving forward in a relationship that we believed may not have been God's plan for him, a confirmation. And to solidify this principle, and steer the conversation to speaking about our own sins, we each began sharing a few of our own errors that had taught us more than if someone had stopped us from learning the lesson the hard way. Very quickly my son was no longer concerned, but agreed that the Lord was in control and realized the blessings of getting out of the way of others—who may even be headed for trouble.

What about you?

Are you convinced that to get in the way of others is your duty? Or can you now see it only slows the process of repentance while also entangling you, stealing your joy?

But what if the person is headed toward sin and you know they will soon become entangled and weighted down by all sorts of encumbrances? After what we've learned, will you continue to get yourself entangled rather than giving it to the Lord, allowing God to use it for their good? How many entanglements have you already gotten caught in that are *not* your own?

True, though these potential entanglements many times are excellent for "teaching what is good" to those who ask, once you've shared the truth, are you always able to step back and let them follow the truth once you shared it, even if they choose to ignore the truth?

So often I find that many people will immediately embrace the truth, but never act on it, as it says will happen in Matthew 13:20, "The one on whom seed was sown on the rocky places, this is the man who hears the word and immediately receives it with joy; yet he has no firm root in himself, but is only temporary…" Allow God to break up the rocky soil in the hearts of the people around you. When we do it they resent us. Yet, if we allow God to do it, we can be there when they're broken, helping to encourage them to accept the Lord's love— but only if we are continually bathing in His love.

Today I realize I am just beginning to understand that it is not enough to just lay my own sins and encumbrances aside, I must also be determined to purposely not get caught in the webs of other people's lives, including and especially those who are closest and most loved. The ongoing and enormous problems of my own life, all that I have been living through recently, have again been working out for good: They have helped me to fully step away from entangling myself with others, leaving them to be led by the Lord or experience the consequences of their sins—ultimately when we all learn more from having gone through it. So, just as I've been doing with my own problems or concerns, I will now happily give all the problems or concerns I have for others to my Beloved Husband who is just as concerned for my loved one's as He is for me!

Yes, problems may continue to surround me, but I choose to give them to the One who has the power and wisdom to deal with them. This frees me up, once again, to simply snuggle into His arms, and marvel at His love. "This is my beloved and this is my Friend" (Song of Solomon 5:16).

Chapter 13

Those Voices

Because I feared the **people**
and listened to their **voice**.
—1 Samuel 15:24

Is there any one of us who has not been swayed by what other people have said to us? I doubt that any of us are so well-grounded and close enough with the Lord that what is said to or about us has absolutely no effect on how we feel or what we ultimately do as a result of other people's opinions.

You may have a mother or father, boss or husband, or even ex-boss or ex-husband whose words continually bombard your mind giving unrest to your soul. For some unknown reason, we automatically embrace hurtful words and choose to believe them—even if the person comes back later to retract what they said. People often blurt out cutting words when they are hurt or frustrated. Unfortunately, because we believe that they meant what they said, we're *choosing* to hang on to what inevitably weighs us down and steals our joy. What's the remedy?

Wounds that Festered

Years ago I was in the midst of such a terrible spiritual battle that had been deeply established within my marriage. My husband (at the time) was struggling (as he always had) with self-worth. When anyone you know or love struggles with this problem of not feeling worthy, it is often remedied by that person putting you (and other people) down shamelessly in order to feel better about themselves.

For what seemed like the umpteenth time, my husband sat me down for almost an hour condemning me for not following the book that I was teaching from, *A Wise Woman,* and what the group of women I was teaching would think if they *really* knew me. It was after that umpteenth time, that I *finally* took what he said to the Lord and asked Him if it was true. I never ever had questioned the validity of it, simply assuming my husband was right. Wow, was I wrong. What I heard was totally different and it literally changed my life. It helped to silence the words that normally would be replayed over and over again in my own head, making me doubt if I should really be ministering to other women.

You know, my Darling, that **when we hear the truth it always silences the lies.** That is why we must take whatever we hear (especially a bad report about ourselves) to the Lord and talk to Him about it—not waiting until it's done immeasurable damage, but right away, immediately. The truth is, we know it's rooted in the enemy who's made it his mission to steal, kill and destroy us—so making us feel worthless and undeserving is in his wheelhouse right? So he uses those he's already wounded and **enslaved**, having them spew out unkind and cutting words he continually feeds them, and then we listen—choosing to believe lies as truth. "Do you not know when you present yourselves to someone as *slaves* of obedience, you are *slaves* of the one whom you obey, either of *sin resulting in death*, or of obedience resulting in righteousness?" (Romans 6:16).

So why do we continue to play into this web of destruction when our Beloved is just longing to be gracious to us? Since almost all of what is said that hurts us, is actually rooted in the deep hurts of that other person.

What the Lord did that day was so precious, something I've never forgotten. He asked me one-by-one if I followed a chapter, beginning with the last chapter of the *Wise Woman* workbook. He asked me if I followed what it said regarding teaching my own children. I had to reply sheepishly, "Yes." Next was whether or not I trusted the Lord with my fertility, when He reminded me that I had even risked death, twice, by not following the doctors (who would have jumped to do a hysterectomy when I was hemorrhaging). I replied, "Yes" once again. One-by-one He continued asking me about each chapter, until He asked me if He was my First Love (Chapter 2). Of course I was thrilled to say, "Oh Yes!!" Then, He ended by asking, "Where is your life (and home) built Michele?" I had to answer, "On You and You alone! My Rock."

Dear bride, from the moment I heard the truth, that instant, all those horrid condemning voices in my head were silenced. Yes, the accusations actually continued, but only for a short time, and I believe it's because it no longer affected or rattled me. As a matter of fact, instead of feeling badly or ashamed of myself, when he'd sit me down, I felt only compassion. How horrible for anyone who feels the need to put someone else down all because of feeling so badly about themselves.

Looking back, it's really not all that surprising, because at the time we were near the end of our marriage, and I, of course, didn't know he was deeply into adultery. So as a pastor, I'm sure the enemy was bombarding him with all sorts of condemnation and shame—tearing away at him. Sadly, as it is throughout the church, he was never taught to take these "negative" emotions to the Lord, asking Him for the truth. Had he done so, maybe he would have felt convicted by his sin, while at the same time, feeling His tremendous love. This, I believe can get any of us out of the deepest of sins and heal our wounds, His love.

Epidemic

Dear bride, I know that I am not the only one who is living with those negative voices. Just this past week I had the privilege of sharing a few hours with one of my beloved WW group members, who is also one of our church leaders (and who used to work under me). She told me that while I was still working at the church, the enemy had been bombarding her mind, telling her that if *I only knew* what she was really like, I would tell our senior pastor, suggesting he ask her to step down from her position. Wow, it seems that this is one tactic that the enemy loves to use—probably because it works so well!!

Then, soon after this, I had the same sort of email from two other church leaders—saying if I really knew what they were like I wouldn't want to associate with them. And each time I was stunned.

Then shortly after He showed me it's not just women here, but it's the same all over the world. Within a few minutes after landing in Africa, while driving away from the airport, one of my longest and dearest friends (and who's also a RMI leader working with Erin), turned to me, taking a deep sigh, then bolstered all her courage to confess, "what she was really like." I listened, knowing this confession had been held back for years. Then, when she finished, all I could do was to lean over to hug her and tell her I struggled with the very same things.

Darling bride, the truth is, we all struggle with the very same things; isn't that what the Bible says? "No temptation has overtaken you but such as is **common** to [wo]man; and God is faithful, who will not allow you to be tempted beyond what you are able, but with the temptation will provide the *way of escape* also, that you may be able to *endure* it" (1 Corinthians 10:13).

Then to prevent this onslaught of cutting words that have become so common, we also need to keep in mind this verse—which really helped me discern whether I should ignore something or take it to heart. "Finally brethren, whatever is *true*, whatever is *honorable*, whatever is *right*, whatever is *pure*, whatever is *lovely*, whatever is of good report; if there is any **virtue** and if there is any praise, think on these things" (Philippians 4:8).

This means, only IF what's said is: honorable, right, pure, lovely, it's **true** (which means we must always remember to go to Him to see if it's the truth), *and* it also needs to be something you want to praise God for. And if it's not all these things, then don't let it enter your heart because whatever is being said is not from Him.

Use every vicious word for good, giving you the opportunity to spend deeper times with Him. Simply remember and make it a habit to take each and every question you have about anything, no matter what it is, to the Lord. Ask Him to let you know what He thinks about it. Then sit quietly to listen, and feel drenched in His love, which you can turn around, and shower on everyone around you.

——— Chapter 14 ———

You're Beautiful!!

"If you do not know,
most beautiful of women . . .
How beautiful you are, my darling!
Oh, how beautiful!"
—Song of Solomon 1:8, 15

Maybe I have shared this before, but a lot of those words that hurt us, which we were talking about in the last chapter, are words or thoughts rehearsed in our minds that deal with the way we look. Today, more than ever, some of us are continually bombarded by thoughts of how we fail to look and really *feel* pretty. We believe we are either: too fat or too thin, too tall or too short, our noses are too long or too wide, our skin is either too white or too dark—the list is endless.

While traveling to different parts of the world, when I arrived in Brazil, I was surprised by what I saw. Brazil appears to be even more obsessed (even more than the U.S.) about women feeling the need to look and feel sexy. Before even leaving the airport, as I was standing, waiting at the luggage carousel, I noticed that I was the only woman who did not have a lot of skin showing. My stomach and cleavage was covered, and my clothes were not really tight nor provocative.

My astonishment continued as my host family drove me through the city to the church where I was invited to speak. I was mesmerized by all the billboards that shouted this trend in their society; there were extremely sexy ads of women everywhere. The craziest aspect of this and what had me dumbfounded was these Brazilian women are simply gorgeous!! So why do they feel the need to show any more than their beautiful faces and lovely figures in whatever clothing made them feel pretty? As I sat puzzled, I remembered seeing a television special that said that South America had the most Miss

Universe winners than any other continent, and in one country most girls are sent to schools to teach them how to win the title by grooming them with how they talk, walk, what to wear, etc. It seems that no matter how gorgeous we are, most of us *feel* inferior; myself included.

So a few weeks later, while flying to another continent, I had plenty of time to talk to the Lord about this. I began by asking Him for a way to explain to women all over the world just how He saw them. What's interesting is, I was on my way to Africa, where my host family had set up a time for us to go on a safari. And that's when I *really* understood just how what He had said meant to me, which I hope to convey to each of you. And I'd like you each to promise to encourage at least one other woman you meet or you know, who needs to know just how beautiful she is, about how He sees her—maybe using this same analogy He shared with me.

What the Lord said is that He sees each of us as endangered and who needs protecting, just like all the endangered animals throughout the world. What He'd explained while on my flight, I then saw firsthand when we were driving through the vast expanse of open land, while on safari. When we stopped in the protected and fenced rest areas, I met people who'd come from all parts of the world for one reason only—just to strain to get a look at even one of these animals. Say, for instance, the gorgeous and majestic giraffe. Yet, while this sweet giraffe is being admired and photographed, the Lord said, to have me imagine herself thinking, "Just look at me. Why does my neck have to be so long? How embarrassing that I have to spread my legs apart just to get a drink of water! And all these brown spots . . . why can't I have that gorgeous coat like that Miss Leopard over there!"

Then along walks an incredible and highly endangered rhino who says, "I can't believe I got my mother's long nose, it's so embarrassing, and her overly large rear-end too—it's huge! Why does my skin have to be this dark and leathery, why can't it be soft like Miss Leopard?"

And there we were, driving hours, doing our best to take pictures of every angle of the rhino, whether it's her large bottom or hoping to get that snapshot of her side view to show the beautiful length of that nose! We only hope to see a giraffe drinking from a watering hole, with her legs spread due to her long legs and long neck, thrilled if we ever can get close enough to see the long black tongue—taking pictures and pictures to later show everyone we know.

Hopefully, you get the picture.

Our own opinions of how we look is not at all how the Lord looks at any one of us. To Him, as He said, we are all on His endangered list since there are no two of us who are just alike! Our Beloved loves our side view, our hair, our skin shade and texture, even the imperfections we believe we see in our looks. The Lord loves how tall we are or how short. He even likes that extra weight that we've put on. Just imagine seeing a skinny animal and how horrified and heartbroken we would be if we saw one.

Since weight seems to be an obsession in most women, if you struggle like most of us, and are currently heavier than you'd like to be, I spoke to Him about that too! Here's how He assured me that no matter how much I weigh, I'm still beautiful. While I was in Italy, I instantly noticed that the greatest and most famous artists painted and sculpted very large, curvy women! Even their backsides were considered beautiful when quite large and full. Yet here we are playing right into the hands of the enemy who loves to make us *feel* as if we fall short of being beautiful. By whose standards? Not the Lord's. And why should we care about our outer beauty anyway when we know that "Charm is deceitful and **beauty is *vain*,** but a woman who *fears the Lord, she shall be praised"* (Proverbs 31:30)? If it's becoming older that's troubling you, He even reminded me of 2 Corinthians 4:16-18, "Therefore we do not lose heart, but though our outer man is decaying, yet our inner man is being renewed day by day." And in the Amplified version it says even more. "Therefore we do not become discouraged [spiritless, disappointed, or afraid]. Though our outer self is [progressively] wasting away, yet our inner self is being [progressively] renewed day by day. For our momentary, light distress [this passing trouble] is producing for us an eternal weight of glory [a fullness] beyond all measure [surpassing all comparisons, a transcendent splendor and an endless blessedness]! So we look not at the things which are seen, but at the things which are unseen; for the things which are visible are temporal [just brief and fleeting], but the things which are invisible are **everlasting *and imperishable*.**"

When I shared all of this with the ladies in South Africa, one precious member told me later that the next morning she stood and looked at herself in the mirror and said, she actually liked what she saw. For the first time she was looking through the eyes of her Beloved! A few weeks later I shared it again at a conference in Nairobi, Kenya where women had traveled from many countries all over the continent of Africa. Though I wasn't there long enough to speak to anyone afterwards, I saw the message transform them when I looked into each of their faces. The Lord had me look around the audience and I could see faces beaming with joy and some women had tears streaming down their faces. All I'd done was ask Him His opinion along with a way to explain it to other women, then made sure I also asked for an opportunity to share what He'd told me, what I had taken the time to ask the Lord to help me do—and dear bride, you can do the same thing too! Take what I've shared, if it has touched you, and share it with other women, let them each know how HE sees us. Then continue this each and every time you have a need or hurt or question. Take it to Him, listen to how He explains it to you, then pass this loving message to women after you ask Him to show you who needs to hear it.

Pretty Muscular

Something new I felt I needed to add. In just the last few years another phenomenon has taken me by surprise, which is the trend for women to work out or train to the point of looking as muscular as a young man. In Erin's *Wise Woman* book, she taught me about how important it was for celebrating how we were created male and female. Then she explained the danger of how blurring these lines has contributed to homosexuality.

Rather than women wanting to *feel* and look pretty, I now see that women today strive, instead, to look pretty muscular. Not only does this excessive training with weights and exercises produce well-defined and bulky muscles, which were once reserved for men, but when women train to this extent, it often reduces the breast tissue and can actually stop a woman's monthly cycle. Is this honoring and celebrating how we were created, female? Would an overly muscular woman be easily viewed as His bride and feel as He intended?

It's not to say we need to be ashamed if we were created more muscular or masculine, but only if we strive to be more the way the world is changing—to blend the male and female genders. It not only robs you of feeling pretty, the way He sees us, but it is also getting dangerously close to the slippery slope of a society that goes beyond accepting who a person is. It now promotes a way of living contrary to the Abundant Life—enjoying being who we were created to be, a woman, His bride.

How He Sees You

While in Brazil I had one hostess who continually said to me, "Linda, linda, linda" that means "Beautiful, beautiful, beautiful." Precious one, that's what your Lover, your Heavenly Husband, says each time He looks at you! He just can't keep His eyes off of you, and His love grows with each glance. There is no need to work out, or change who you are, since you are Linda, His beautiful, bride, "If you do not know, most beautiful of women . . . How beautiful you are, my darling! Oh, how beautiful!" (Song of Solomon 1:8, 15).

———— Capítulo 15 ————

Utterly Lovesick

"My beloved is mine, and I am His . . .
When I found Him whom my soul loves;
I held on to Him and would not let Him go . . .
For I am lovesick."
—Song of Solomon 3:2–4; 5:8

When I began this chapter, uncharacteristically thanks to His love, I struggled to get it written. I knew where we were headed, and I also knew that it was fear that was causing my hesitancy. Though we've been told 365 times in the Bible never to fear anything, and as I've written before, especially not fearing what other people think, I still had hesitated and put off writing this chapter. My concern was that I knew what I had to say had the potential to stir up fearful emotions in some of you who are currently seeking restoration for their marriage, then potentially be used by the enemy to discourage you.

At the same time, what I'm about to share is so exciting from my perspective, I literally want to shout it from the rooftops, telling the entire world. So no matter how it begins to unfold, my desire in writing this chapter is to help you understand it was your heart I had in mind. It is my hope that it will not, in anyway, make you feel in the least discouraged or worried or that any other negative emotion would wash over you.

The way it can adversely affect you is that so often we see the journeys others are called to take and we can't help but wonder, "How is this going to affect me? Is this something He is going to make me go through too?" The truth is, most often the answer is, No, and He's not going to call you to take the same course He's asked me (or others) to take. So anytime you start to become concerned, stop to let His love and assurance quiet your fears because there's simply no way His plan for your future is not intended to be bright, exciting and drenched in His love. Remember, He died to give you your Abundant Life, right?!

So, to get started, please bear with me just a bit longer because I'm going to veer off before I begin. It's because just recently I was reading a book by an author and I found myself so lost with almost half of what she'd written. It was because she'd written it with her "regular followers" or fans in mind, and I was not one of them—so I had no idea what she was even talking about. So this means that I need to begin this chapter by quickly laying out my personal situation, so that those of who are new to my books or to Erin's RMI ministry are not confused by what I am about to share.

One of the most difficult parts of going through my husband leaving and divorcing me, once again, had to do with the fact that my personal ministering and also helping RMI originated with my own marriage being restored. After years of seeking God to restore my marriage, He answered my prayers, when I trusted God to restore it, while learning and diligently following the restoration principles that I found from RMI, which I readily confirmed by checking them with my own Bible. As a result, soon after my marriage was restored, women in my church came to me for help and guidance that resulted in me having a ministry within my church. Then later it also opened doors for me to speak around the world—bringing hope to women who were in marriage crises and unbearable pain who also wanted their marriage restored.

"Then the LORD stretched out His hand and touched my mouth, and the LORD said to me, 'Behold, I have put My words in your mouth. See, I have appointed you this day over the nations and over the kingdoms, to pluck up and to break down, to destroy and to overthrow, to build and to plant" (Jeremiah 1:9–10).

So when my husband had once again left me, and divorced me after fourteen years of being restored (who, I shared was one of the pastors at the church where I'd been ministering), many women bailed out of our fellowships as quickly as they would if a ship was sinking—but who could blame them? Those who remained were left stunned, shocked, and shaken as they couldn't help but think of their own marriage and they were afraid their restoration wouldn't "last" either. Surprisingly, many expected *me* to give *them* encouragement and support during a time in my own life when I was living through it, which left me also a bit bewildered, because I had no idea what was really up ahead for me, or my ministry, or my children, or my finances, or my future.

As strange as it sounds, that's when He began opening the doors for me to begin to travel (actually just three weeks after my divorce was final). I got invitations from several churches, where they said they had many women who had questions regarding how this would change their restoration. And, one of the most sought after questions had to do with inquiries about *my future* "marriage restoration"— when and how it would take place "this time." What I learned from coming through my husband's second abandonment, (and you'll understand more if you read my book *Facing Divorce—Again*), was that a crisis of this magnitude has a way of changing its victim in incredible ways. It's actually not only brought me to a level of intimacy that I only ever dreamed I would have with the Lord; but it was a deeper intimacy than I thought even existed or had ever remotely heard anyone ever share, not even something I'd heard someone sing about.

This newly enhanced relationship I'd found very soon became the main focus of my life. I no longer was looking at my future or any other detail of life, certainly not about any sort of marriage restoration. Wonderfully, my attention turned solely to the One whom I found loved me beyond imagination. When this happened, I realized that I was desperate to hold onto His tenderness towards me no matter what. The desperation began to actually become an obsession especially when I felt it threatened. Anytime I would get an email or was asked by someone "Michele I'm excited to know when your next restoration might take place? Has God told you how it's going happen?" When anyone would ask me about my future restoration with my ex-husband, I found myself digging deeper into the heart of my Beloved lest anyone try to take me away from what I had found— HIM and His love. Love that I was soaking in, each day, every day, and especially resting in throughout the night.

During these times I felt threatened, when I'd asked Him to never let me go, He often lead me to read, "The woman who is unmarried, and the virgin, is concerned about the things of the Lord, that she may be holy both in body and spirit; *but* one who is **married** is concerned about the things of the world, *how she may please her husband.* This I say for your own benefit; not to put a restraint upon you, but to promote what is appropriate and to secure **undistracted devotion to the Lord**...*But in my opinion she is **happier if she** remains as she is; and I think that I also have the Spirit of God"* (1 Corinthians 7: 34–40).

At first when I'd answer any question regarding my next or second marriage restoration, I found myself basically on autopilot or sort of in a daze. What I struggled with had to do with my ministering. For years I'd been working with Erin to help women who were desperate (as I had been) to have their marriages restored, so of course at the time this was my main and only focus for what I ministered.

So, with the turn of events in my life, very quickly I knew that even though I could surely lose my position with RMI and also lose my entire fellowship that I'd established at my church, along with any further speaking engagements (and which meant losing any and all my income, that was already crumbling beneath me), I felt I needed to be completely transparent and share my true feelings—I no longer was seeking restoration, and in fact, I did not want it.

"My beloved is mine, and I am His . . . When I found Him whom my soul loves; I held on to Him and would not let him go . . . **For I am lovesick"** (Song of Solomon 3:2–4; 5:8).

At the time this was going on, this concept had never ever been spoken about within the ministry, but thankfully, no longer is a statement about it (not wanting my marriage restored) as shocking as it once had been. Unfortunately, since I had been the first to utter such heresy, I watched as many women began to turn their backs on me. The new focus of my ministry was more than they could bear, and sadly they wrongly began to believe that I no longer *believed* in marriage restoration since I wasn't seeking it for myself.

My dilemma wore on and at one point, early one morning while still in bed, I blurted out to the Lord that I would obey and do *anything* He asked me, but... I would **not** restore my marriage to my ex-husband because I would never leave Him! I pulled the covers over my head, and within seconds I began to weep thinking of how I must have grieved my Husband with my horrid attitude. With tears, I sobbed, asking if He was disappointed in me. What I heard surprised me, and I believe it will surprise you too. He said that it did not grieve Him in anyway, but instead it blessed Him and touched His heart!!

Stunned, He went on by reminding me how Joshua rebelled against God's command to stay off Mt. Zion (since anyone who came too close would be killed) while Moses went up to meet with Him face-to-face. Joshua wanted and needed more of God—no matter what it cost him. Then later, did you remember it was Joshua who took over when Moses's anger caused him to never make it to the Promised Land? So what he'd done, going against God's command, was rewarded.

Next He reminded me about Ruth and when she refused Naomi's insistence to leave her and go back to her people. Ruth demanded saying, no, she would remain with her mother-in-law—and that's when God blessed her and she became the wife of Boaz—not to mention being in the lineage of Jesus!

Next the Lord reminded me about Elisha who refused each time Elijah tried to make him stay behind. God blessed him as we see later in the Bible that it was Elisha who had far more of an anointing, more than Elijah ever had.

It seems that God is pleased with undying loyalty, devotion, and a kind of love that refuses to leave His presence.

Even though I felt much better, I still found myself so anxious and fearful that the Lord would someday ask me to restore my marriage with my ex-husband, possibly for His glory. Then one fateful day while in South Africa, my dear, sweet hostess asked me if she could ask me a personal question. When she asked, it was basically the same sort of question that seemed to be on everyone's mind, "Would you ever take your husband back?" I answered her the same way as I'd done countless times before:

"No matter what God asked me to do, I would do . . . no matter what it was."

That night as I lay in bed, I did something that seems so simple, yet I had never thought about it until then. I asked the Lord, "Darling, when someone asks me *that* question, how do *You* want me to answer?"

What I heard Him say left me baffled; He said, "Just tell them that **you can't.**"

For the next few weeks many Bible verses began to run through my mind as I was desperately trying to make sense of what He had told me. What did He mean when He said, ". . . you can't"?

With no verse or principle coming to my mind, I woke up eager to begin searching throughout my Bible to find verses to help me understand. But that morning I was heading to Kenya and I didn't have my favorite Bible with me. When I began traveling extensively, I stopped bringing it because it got slightly damaged on one trip, so while traveling, I relied on my laptop Bible that I connect to on the internet. (This was prior to having the luxury of a Bible app on your phone and internet wherever you are in the world.)

While looking back, it's almost laughable now, because He'd told me the night I hurriedly boarded my plane for Kenya, and that's a country where the Internet was almost impossible to connect to. Where I was staying had no internet, and there was only one internet café where you could buy a few minutes, which I used up to stay connected to my children. Why had He orchestrated telling me without having the ability to search? Because the Lord just wanted me to be quiet and seek Him; time to simply sit still, listening to what He wanted to tell me Himself.

What I heard you'll be reading in the next chapter. But just as the Lord had me disconnect from searching elsewhere, He's asked me to leave you, too, to give you time to just be still and let the Lord speak to you. Don't just stop for a few minutes before reading the next chapter, instead, take a few days, or longer, to allow the Lord to speak to you regarding what He told me and what He's going to have me share. I believe He's about to open your heart, allowing you to begin living the abundant life of your dreams!

Remember, "God can do anything, you know—far more than you could ever imagine or guess or request in your wildest dreams!" (Ephesians 3:20 The Message).

"Therefore the LORD longs to be gracious to you, and therefore He WAITS on high to have compassion on you. For the LORD is a God of justice; how blessed are all those who long for Him" (Isaiah 30:18).

———————— Capítulo 16 ————————

No Longer an Adulteress

"So then, if while her husband is living
she is joined to another man,
she shall be called an **adulteress**;
but if her husband dies, she is free from the law,
so that she is not an **adulteress**
though she is joined to another man."
—Romans 7:3

Dear Michele,

Hi, my name is Anita and I am a member of Restoration Ministries International. I read your Bible study today and I feel I have to share something the Lord has led me to in His Word concerning a certain part of the "Wise Woman Study," specifically, "I Hate Divorce!" Something I think you must have missed. This is something the Lord had shown me quite some time ago and I know I have written about it before. It concerns the part "Should I restore this marriage or go back to my first husband?" under "An Adulterous Foundation." It is in Deuteronomy; please pay particular attention to verse four as this is my concern for which I write to you this morning.

Deuteronomy 24:1-4 KJV, "When a man hath taken a wife, and married her, and it come to pass that she find no favour in his eyes, because he hath found some uncleanness in her: then let him write her a bill of divorcement, and give it in her hand, and send her out of his house.

And when she is departed out of his house, she may go and be another man's wife. And if the latter husband hate her, and write her a bill of divorcement, and giveth it in her hand, and sendeth her out of his

house; or if the latter husband die, which took her to be his wife;
verse 4 *Her former husband, which sent her away, may not take her
again to be his wife, after that she is defiled; for that is abomination
before the LORD: and thou shalt not cause the land to sin, which the
LORD thy God giveth thee for an inheritance."*

I hope this is helpful and will prompt you to change your direction.
Thank you for listening. I've appreciated your helping so many of us
understand the true Word of the Lord when so many of us are so
desperately in need! GOD WILL NOT LET IT GO UNNOTICED;
ALL OF YOUR LABOR OF LOVE! Peace in the Lord!

~ Anita

When I got this email I wrote to my secretary and asked if she'd
respond with, "Can you write to Anita and tell her I totally agree with
the verse and her opinion? Also let her know that I will prayerfully
consider what she has shared and will seek the Lord about it, then
speak to Erin," which I did.

What Erin and I discussed was that the main reason Erin left that
portion in *A Wise Woman* is because it has always been her desire that
all women seek the Lord concerning her own personal situation since
each of our relationships with the Lord is the most important thing in
anyone's life—even more important than a woman's marriage.

My life, like yours, has without any doubt been a journey, and like
me, very often we have thought about the mistakes in our past that we
each, later, found clearly in Scripture that we had been wrong. At that
point in time, when I was personally reading and teaching *A Wise
Woman*, I never really understood of that particular principle, a
principle that had caused me to make this "mistake" and what many
other women began to challenge me about soon after Anita did. All I
could do was wonder how I'd missed it.

Darling bride, have you ever felt that way? Wondering how or why
God didn't stop you or open your eyes to something before it took
you on a journey that, looking back, you would rather have missed
living through? Painfully realizing that due to this misstep, that could
have been avoided, you are suffering the consequences of due to

being so ignorant? It wasn't prior to you knowing the Lord or prior to knowing His word. It was almost like He pointed you in the wrong direction.

My Plan

"I don't think the way you think. The way you work isn't the way I work. For as the sky soars high above earth, so the way I work surpasses the way you work, and the way I think is beyond the way you think" (Isaiah 55:8-11: The Message).

Just recently, specifically on a recent traveling tour that took me through South America, Africa, and Europe which I am only two days from completing, I found myself asking the Lord about many of my "mistakes." Why I had made them, and more pointedly, why my Beloved had not stopped me from making them. To my incredible surprise He told me that these were not mistakes, but each were part of His plan for my life! So I stopped to ponder long what He'd just said. As each "mistake" came to my mind, the outcome, especially on some of my most regrettable mistakes, had turned out to be the ones that brought me closer to my Lord, my Lover, my Husband and my Best Friend. So, I thought, if this is what our mistakes do for us, I then began to finally comprehend that there is never any reason for any of us to regret our past, and that means never having to worry about our future, worrying about any mistakes we could make.

This revelation held immeasurable truth for me, and I also finally understood it's what "Perfect love that casts out all fear" really meant! Just imagine no longer being fearful of making mistakes—so we become free and are able to let go of all our worries. Finally, with all fear gone, we can freely love Him as He deserves to be loved—for loving Him is the reason for our entire existence. And when you couple your future with the knowledge that any mistakes we make are intended to be used for our good, along with all the mistakes of our past (that we once felt we couldn't let go of), we are finally free to enjoy living the Abundant Life that He died to give us!

In that moment, no longer plagued with the guilt and weight of being divorced, and why I had remarried, I was now free to simply love:

love and be loved by my new Husband; love and be loved by my children; love and be loved by everyone else the Lord puts on my heart—and it is the same for you too!

No, I have not forgotten that I said this would be a continuation of the previous chapter, when I left you hanging with trying to understand what the Lord meant when He told me that "you can't" in regard to restoring my marriage to my ex-husband. Many of you may have already been able to figure out why "I can't" when you read the opening verse:

"So then, if while her husband is living she is joined to another man, she *shall be called an adulteress;* but if her husband dies, she is free from the law, so that she is *not* an **adulteress** though she is joined to another man" (Romans 7:3).

Since my first husband and my second husband are both still alive, if I were to restore my marriage (which would mean me marrying my ex-husband a second time, since I am divorced), then I would be an adulteress—again!

Yes, again. For all those years, those very difficult and painful years of marriage, I was nothing more than an adulteress. My first marriage lasted only one month, my second marriage to my ex-husband was a long and laborious struggle for nearly 24 years—years of his unfaithfulness and my misery, as I tried desperately to be a different wife, a woman worthy to be loved by him.

Then, with the log in my own eye, I tried to take the speck out of all those OWs who had stolen our husbands. To my surprise, when the Lord revealed the state of my own existence, that I was living as an adulteress, all of it began to make sense. The years of feeling unloved by my husband, who left me twice for other women, was all about me, never about him. Maybe that is why I never felt anything but compassion for the woman that my husband recently married—I knew that if not for the grace of God, I too, would be looking for another man to marry me after being rejected, which ultimately would result in another failed marriage and me being an adulteress, again.

For all those years I'd lived as an adulteress and didn't even know it. Yes, true, our society recognizes divorce as ending an unwanted marriage, and then accepts remarriage as legal; however, even in Erin's books (I taught and ministered with), I was blind to the Bible verses like:

"So then, if while her husband is living she is joined to another man, she *shall be called an adulteress;* but if her husband dies, she is free from the law, so that she is *not* an **adulteress** though she is joined to another man" (Romans 7:3).

"But I say to you that everyone who divorces his wife, except for the cause of unchastity, makes *her commit adultery;* and whoever marries a divorced woman **commits adultery"** (Matthew 5:32).

Since my first husband divorced me, and then I married a second time, I therefore, commit adultery (since my first husband *was* living). Though I never saw it that way, we both reaped the consequences nevertheless.

"To keep you from the evil woman, from the **smooth tongue** of the adulteress. Do not desire her beauty in your heart, do not let her catch you with her eyelids. For on account of a harlot one is **reduced to a loaf of bread,** and an adulteress hunts for the precious life. Can a man take fire to his bosom, and his clothes not be burned? The one who commits adultery with a woman *is lacking sense;* he who would destroy himself does it. Wounds and disgrace he will find, and his reproach will not be blotted out" (Proverbs 6:24–33).

Financially, while married, we had always struggled. In addition, how true that "wounds and disgrace" did find my husband and that "reproach" was never blotted out. Back when I first found RMI, the Lord did open my eyes, just a bit, concerning this principle when I was seeking God to restore my marriage. While reading these verses I realized that it was *me* who had caused my husband (at the time) to commit adultery, since I had been married before when I married him. About half way in my restoration journey, late one evening when he had come to visit our small children, I repented and told him, "I know that everyone is looking at you because you are living with this other woman and committing adultery, but I am the one who made you an adulterer, so they should look at me and blame me" and pointed to this verse, "But I say to you that everyone who divorces his wife, except for the cause of unchastity, makes *her commit adultery*; and whoever marries a divorced woman **commits adultery"** (Matthew 5:32).

So strange that I never thought for one single moment, not then nor when we remarried after our divorce when He restored us, that to marry him again would mean that I, once again, would be living in adultery. I did have other people tell me that I would be, but that only made me feel condemned, and that they were judging me legalistically, knowing I was under His grace. So now do you understand why God never revealed this truth to my heart or opened my eyes to this principle? And quite possibly why you're newly discovering errors you've made that He never prevented you from making?

It is because we are all on a journey. A journey of growing, learning and becoming wise. We are not born wise, with all knowledge or understanding, and therefore, I believe that not all of God's principles are we able to absorb or are able to grasp because it's not yet time to. It's the same with our children: young children are unable to grasp their nakedness, just as if they were still living in the Garden of Eden. You can tell them that they shouldn't walk around unclothed, and you do your best to cover them up, but it does no good until they are able to grasp and understand this truth.

During the time of my own ignorance to being an adulteress, God worked it all out for good, not just for me, but for so many others. Isn't that amazing? In my ignorance God blessed me with a ministry and also 2 restoration babies born after my I was restored— even though I ignorantly had entered back into adultery.

Maybe you're not convinced, and you believe that for me to remarry my ex-husband again would be okay, that the blood of Jesus covers my sin, because He'd done it before. Actually I agree that His blood does cover the sin, any sin. However, He no longer wants me to live with the *consequences* of being an adulteress. In addition, I believe for me to enter into remarriage, now that my eyes are open to the truth, would mean I would not be just transgressing—I would be entering into sin willfully. As Erin wrote in one of her books, this also applies to me:

"For if we go on sinning willfully after receiving the knowledge of the truth, there no longer remains a sacrifice for sins. How much more **severe a punishment** do you think he will deserve who has trampled underfoot the Son of God. Vengeance is mine, I will repay. The Lord will judge His people. *It is a **terrifying thing** to fall into the hands of the living God"* (Hebrews 10:26–31).

And, "This is the way of an adulterous woman: she eats and wipes her mouth, and says, '**I have done nothing wrong**'" (Proverbs 30:20).

Finally, "A wife is bound as long as her husband lives; but if her husband is dead, **she is free to be married** to whom she wishes, only in the Lord" (1 Corinthians 7:39). This means, for me to remarry now would mean that both my first and second husband would have to be deceased. Unless of course it was something He told me to do.

Would He, could He ask someone to do something that was wrong? Actually, I did ask, and that's when He reminded me about Hosea, and for him as a priest to marry Gomer, a publically know adulteress, "Then the Lord said to me [Hosea], 'Go again, love a woman who is loved by her husband, yet an adulteress'" (Hosea 3:1). Many speculate about whether or not Gomer married another man after leaving Hosea, but I believe the message is the same. Being a priest they were to keep pure, if not, their children (and generations following) would be polluted. Because Hosea had to have known this, being a priest, he knowingly went against what His Word said, listening to what He personally told him to do.

"What about Me?"

Dear, dear, precious one. What I have shared with you in this chapter is my own personal walk to finding freedom: freedom to love and be loved, no longer longing to be loved by someone who *maybe* never even loved me at all. If you feel hopeless and helpless after reading about my journey, maybe because you have been hoping for your second marriage to be restored, please don't despair.

When the Lord speaks to you, when speaking to each of us personally, what He calls you to do will never be a burden or end badly. First, He says, "Take My yoke upon you and learn from Me, for I am **gentle** and humble in heart, and you will find rest for your souls. For My yoke is easy, and My burden is light" (Matthew 11:29–30). And "'For I know the plans that I have for you,' declares the LORD, 'plans for welfare and not for calamity to give you a future and a hope'" (Jeremiah 29:11).

God has called each of us to travel a different, unique, one-of-a-kind journey with His son, our beloved Husband. It was never intended to be traveled alone, because the purpose of taking it, with each valley and difficulty, was to experience His love, a love witnessed by others.

In addition, the journey He's called me to take is not and will never be exactly like yours or anyone else's. Let me give you an example. Very often when I speak to women who have been transformed by His love and bring up the subject about them "ministering," very often the women panic and blurt out they can't speak in front of a bunch of people! Yet ministering has many parts as it says and is explained in 1 Corinthians 12:12-16, "For even as the body is one and yet has many members, and all the members of the body, though they are many, are one body... For the body is not one member, but many. If the foot says, "Because I am not a hand, I am not a part of the body," it is not for this reason any the less a part of the body. And if the ear says, "Because I am not an eye, I am not a part of the body.""

Though I never wanted to, and I never dreamed He'd call me to, He did open the doors for me to speak publically and also to travel. Though traveling may be *your* dream job, traveling (before He called me), was something that was terrifying to me. Yet now, I could never imagine never having met women who live in an entirely different culture, miles away, who I instantly fell in love with, and who intimately became my dearest, closest friends.

This, my dear bride, is why your journey and your future should never be compared to anyone else's. He has designed a perfect future for you, for each one of us, designed as uniquely as He created our fingerprints.

If you are currently seeking restoration for a second marriage, do not let where I am in my journey or what He's led me to do discourage you, and do not attempt to follow in my path. Don't let the consequences I

lived through discourage you either. If I'd listened to others who told me back then I was wrong, I would never have a ministry nor would I have my two daughters!

Also, please remember, this is why we hurt others and ourselves when we look with wonder as we see women who "appear" a certain way. Like if we see a woman who appears to be loved and cherished by her husband and wonder why it wasn't or isn't this way for us. I did this very thing and often found out later that what appeared one way was not at all the reality. And this is also why it's dangerous to follow doctrine when we were designed to develop a close enough relationship with Him, so He would lead us personally, because this is how God designed us to be, with our Husband as His bride traveling through life before meeting with Him face-to-face when we leave this earth.

If I've learned anything it's that God cannot be put in a box, and when we try to through doctrine, He will break out of this limiting mold supernaturally, and show we are wrong. We witnessed this in Jesus' life with His miracles, and even who He chose to heal—never once did He heal anyone the same way twice: sometimes He spoke, sometimes He spit. Sometimes miracles happened instantaneously, and one time it took Jesus two times for the blind man to see. Again, what He was showing us is that we can never put Him or His power in a box or be able to really figure Him out. Instead, He designed us to spend that effort and time pressing our hearts and lives toward His—where we will be free from worry, wondering and fretting—as His loving bride, trusting our Bridegroom for everything, walking hand-in-hand, or having Him carry us when it becomes difficult or we are weary.

"Trust in the LORD with all your heart and do not lean on your own understanding. In all your ways acknowledge Him, and He will make your paths straight" (Proverbs 3:5–6). This verse means that just by "acknowledging" He's right there next to you, without any pleading or begging or lamenting, He will lead you along the straight path as you face your future.

Speaking of your future, many of you may still be hoping that someday you will have children, as you panic watching your biological clock ticking down, even faster as you approach 30 or 40 years old. Right now He is asking you, "Behold, I am the LORD, the God of all flesh; is anything too difficult for Me?" (Jeremiah 32:27). Will you answer Him, "Ah Lord GOD! Behold, You have made the heavens and the earth by Your great power and by Your outstretched arm! **Nothing is too difficult for You"!** (Jeremiah 32:17), or will you instead choose to shrivel up in despair or seek some sort of manmade solution? As a wiser woman, I know that "Strength and dignity are [your] clothing and [you now will] smile at the future" (Proverbs 31:25).

If your concern is not bearing children in the future, but you are instead in a situation similar to mine, can you honestly say that even though you know that He created the heavens and the earth with His great power and out-stretched arm that your longings now for an earthy husband are impossible for Him to handle??

So what do you do now, in the meantime, when you are in the process of waiting?

Precious one, remember the chapter "Longing for Whom?" back in my first book *Finding Your Abundant Life* when it gave proof that to run after the Lord would mean that happiness would run after you? It is truer now than ever dear bride. What is also true is that once you chase after the Lord, and He lets you catch Him—His love will change it all, everything. For there is none like Him, no, not in all this big world.

My darling, once again, your Beloved is on bended knee, He is offering His love and all that is good, as He asks for your hand to become His beloved bride. It is my desire, my ultimate passion and

life's mission that you will answer Him with these words, sweetly tell
Him . . .

My Beloved is mine, and I am His . . . When I found Him whom
my soul loves; I held on to Him and would not let him go . . .
For I am lovesick.
—Song of Solomon 3:2–4; 5:8.

About the Author

Michele Michaels came to Restore Ministries International when she was facing divorce. At the time she was the mother of two small boys. After reading *How God Can and Will Restore Your Marriage* and *A Wise Woman* and she began helping Erin Thiele with her books, soon after they met while each were in Orlando, Florida. Very soon, after Erin visited Michele in her home in California, Michele's marriage was restored.

Almost exactly Fourteen years later, Michele found herself facing divorce again while helping to update and revise a small Facing Divorce booklet for her church. After returning to RMI to Refresh her mind, Michele began to realize He had planned to use this trial for much good. It was during this new chapter in her life when Michele discovered the real reason God allowed another divorce to happen again and what she had been missing: The Abundant Life that she is now living.

Michele's book *Living the Abundant Life* is available on **EncouragingBookstore.com** and also on **Amazon.com**.

Also, if you've found the freedom to love and be loved by your Husband by reading this book, make sure you read Michele's next books *Breaking free from **The Poverty Mentality*** and ***Moving Mountains*** available from these same booksellers.

Also Available

on EncouragingBookstore.com & Amazon.com

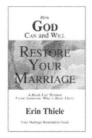
How God Can and Will Restore Your Marriage: From Someone Who's Been There

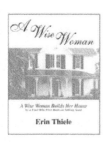
A Wise Woman: A Wise Woman Builds Her House By a FOOL Who First Built on Sinking Sand

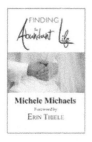
Finding the Abundant Life by Michele Michaels

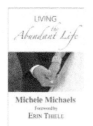
Living the Abundant Life by Michele Michaels

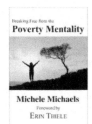 Breaking Free from the Poverty Mentality by Michele Michaels

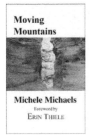 Moving Mountains by Michele Michaels

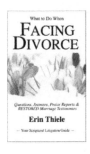 What to Do When Facing Divorce

 Facing Divorce —Again by Michele Michaels

Workers@Home: Making the MOST of Your Time!

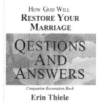

Questions and Answers: How God Will Restore Your Marriage

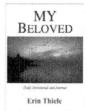

My Beloved: Daily Devotional and Journal

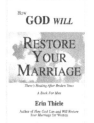

How God Will Restore Your Marriage: There's Healing After Broken Vows — A Book for Men

A Wise Man: A Wise Man Builds Upon a Rock By a FOOL Who Built on Sinking Sand

WOTT Series

Get the full WOTT Series available
on EncouragingBookstore.com & Amazon.com

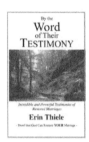

By the Word of Their Testimony (Book 1):
Incredible and Powerful Testimonies of Restored
Marriages

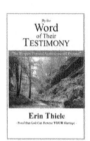

By the Word of Their Testimony (Book 2): No Weapon
Formed Against you will Prosper

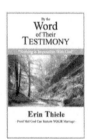

By the Word of Their Testimony (Book 3):
Nothing is Impossible With God

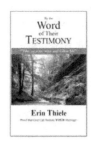

Word of Their Testimony (Book 4): Take up your cross and follow Me

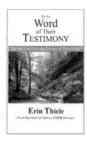

Word of Their Testimony (Book 5): He will Give You the Desires of Your Heart

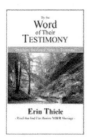

Word of Their Testimony (Book 6): Proclaim the Good News to Everyone

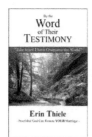

Word of Their Testimony (Book 7): Take Heart! I have Overcome the World

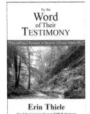

Word of Their Testimony (Book 8): You will have Treasure in Heaven —Come, follow Me

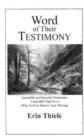

Word of Their Testimony: Incredible and Powerful Testimonies of Restored Marriages From Men

Restore Ministries International

POB 830 Ozark, MO 65721 USA

For more help
Please visit one of our Websites:

EncouragingWomen.org

HopeAtLast.com

RestoreMinistries.net

RMIEW.com

RMIOU.com

Aidemaritale.com (French)

AjudaMatrimonial.com (Portuguese)

AyudaMatrimonial.com (Spanish)

Pag-asa.org (Tagalog Filipino)

UiteindelikHoop.com (Afrikaans)

ZachranaManzelstva.com (Slovak)

EncouragingMen.org

Where you'll also find FREE Courses for men and women.